DUDE, WHERE'S MY CAR-THARSIS?

A Friendly and Engaging Guide to Talk Therapy

PHIL STARK

ISBN 978-0-578-30084-9

E-book ISBN - 978-0-578-30085-6

Contents

Introduction

What is catharsis, exactly? (Or car-tharsis, for that matter?) The dictionary definition of catharsis is "The process of releasing, and thereby providing relief from, strong or repressed emotions". A less formal definition might be something like "That thing that happens when you're feeling sad but then you have some realization about yourself or your life that makes you feel better". When we are feeling depressed, or angry, or anxious or sad or scared or unhappy, it can seem like there's no hope, like we'll never be happy again. We feel miserable. And we don't want to live miserable lives. We want to release those strong, repressed emotions that are making us miserable and get relief from them. We want catharsis. And that is something we can work to achieve through the process of talk therapy.

This book is a combination of two of my passions: writing and psychology. I'm a screenwriter, with credits including *Dude, Where's My Car?*, *That '70s Show*, and *South Park*. I'm also a therapist, with credits including *Graduate School*, *Clinical Training*, and *Private Practice*. But before I ever thought about becoming a writer or a therapist, I was a client. I went to my first therapy session when I was eight years old, and since then I've been in and out of therapy, working through different issues with different therapists at different points in my life. After combining my personal therapy experience with my professional work, I sometimes feel like I've had a lifetime's worth of therapy. And I'm not done yet!

This book is a guide to talk therapy, including what can bring us to it, what we can expect it to be like, and what we can hope to get out of it. It's a collection of concepts I've observed in my time as a therapist, a client, a father, a partner, a son, and a person. It's for people who have never experienced talk therapy and are curious about it, people who have been in talk therapy and are interested learning more about it, and people who see the title and chuckle and buy the book as a gift for someone else who they think might benefit from it.

Many of these chapters present complex concepts through the lens of a metaphor, or other figure of speech, which can help make these concepts more easily understood. The result of this understanding is an increased sense of awareness of the deep rooted emotions that guide us to do what we do, say what we say, and feel how we feel. There is an immense amount of power in this awareness. Without it we repeat the same mistakes, think the same negative thoughts over and over, and continually find ourselves in situations we consider undesirable without any insight as to why we continue to end up there. Awareness alone won't give you the tools to change the things about your life you want to change, but it is the first step in that direction. To change something about yourself, you must first be aware of it!

This book is not a replacement for talk therapy. It is a collection of concepts that come up frequently in therapy, and tools that can help us process these issues in the same way that we would in therapy. However, there's no replacement for actually being in the room (real or virtual) with a trained professional there to help guide you along the way. If any of the chapters in this book resonate with you, and you want to explore the feelings that come up further, I encourage you to reach out to a mental health professional and get the ball rolling on your own personal therapy experience. There's a list of resources at the end of the book to help you with that. But let's not consider the end of the book just yet. We're at the beginning, so let's get started!

ONE

The Quicksand of Depression

M any people who seek therapy suffer from depression in one form or another. Clinically speaking, there are multiple classifications of depression that are categorized in the Diagnostic and Statistical Manual of Mental Disorders (DSM), the handbook used by mental health care providers as a guide to diagnosis. This includes categories like Major Depressive Disorder, Adjustment Disorder, and Dysthymic Disorder, among others. While the difference between these diagnoses involves specifics like the duration and intensity of symptoms, the experience of people suffering from these disorders is similar: Depressed people are sad!

The sadness associated with depression is experienced by people in different ways. Some of us experience depression as a dark mood that lasts a day or two, but not so intense that it impairs our ability to function day to day. For other people depression is a debilitating event that knocks them out of commission and prevents them from functioning normally.

Some people are generally happy but periodically experience bouts of depression and feelings of hopelessness at various points in their lives. Others people report experiencing low levels of depression on a daily basis for as long as they can remember.

Being depressed is like being in quicksand. They're both things that we feel stuck in and struggle to get out of. When you're stuck in depression or quicksand, your movements feel constricted, you find it harder to take action, and simple things that were once easy are now hard to do. The difference is that depression is a mental state while quicksand is a physical one, which affects how the people around you perceive what you are going through. It would be much easier for the people in your life to sympathize what you are experiencing if they could see you stuck in a pit of quicksand, struggling to get out. Depression is not as easily visible. Most of the struggling takes place unseen, in our head. In addition, we often don't want to reveal we're depressed. We don't want to let down our guard and be vulnerable. We put on a brave face and go on about our day, but inside the quicksand is dragging us down.

Depression can make it difficult to accomplish the simplest tasks. It can feel like an impossible feat to just get out of bed, similar to the way that quicksand can make something as simple as moving your arms seem impossible. The tricky thing about quicksand is that the more you struggle, the more you sink. The harder you try to get out of it, the deeper you fall into it. So what do the experts say you should do when you find yourself sinking into a pit of quicksand? Stop struggling and float. Which makes sense to me, but in every movie I've seen involving quicksand the people stuck at first seem annoyed, then confused, and eventually they start to panic as they realize the gravity of their situation. They definitely don't stop struggling and float. They flail and struggle as they sink deeper into the quicksand.

Why don't people stuck in quicksand in movies stop struggling and float? Because that would be boring! When you go to the movies you don't want to see Indiana Jones make a choice that ends up solving the problem in a non-dramatic way. You want to see him struggle to escape the quicksand, dangerously close to sinking beneath the surface, until at the last moment his trusty sidekick throws him a snake to grab onto instead of a rope, forcing Indiana to confront his fear of snakes in order to escape certain death (nice touch, Spielberg!).

So what is the real life depression version of stopping the struggle against the quicksand and floating to the surface? It's not being your own worst enemy. It's not beating yourself up about being depressed, which will only amplify the depression and drag you down even deeper. You wake up in the morning feeling depressed. You don't want to get out of bed. Just taking a shower seems like an impossible task. And you feel bad about this. You remember how easy it was in the past to shower, but that right now it's something you simply can't do and you feel ashamed about it. You can't see this depression ever lifting and you wonder what kind of life you're going to live. How will you ever handle something truly hard, like a job or a relationship, if you can't even crawl out of bed? You suck!

This is what it looks like to struggle against depression. It's the emotional equivalent of kicking and flailing as the quicksand / depression feeds off this energy and sucks you down deeper. In this situation, you can't control whether you feel depressed or not. But you can control your attitude about feeling depressed. You can beat yourself up, feel like a failure, a broken person who is incapable of doing the things human beings are supposed to be able to do in life. Or, you can let yourself be depressed. Give yourself permission to feel sad without judging yourself. Everyone gets depressed at some point in their lives. Recognize that this is your time for it. You don't want to get out of bed and take a shower and that's okay. You're depressed! Let yourself feel depressed. Give yourself permission to feel bad. Stop struggling against the depression and just let yourself float.

This kind of advice can be frustrating sometimes because it doesn't give you any checklist items to check off. There's no concrete set of steps you can take to make things change immediately. It will take time, and change will come slowly, but one day you'll wake up and get out of bed and take a hot shower and come out feeling refreshed. It will be a small victory. You'll feel like meeting that friend for coffee instead of staying home by yourself. You'll go for a walk and see a cute dog or a beautiful sunset and smile and feel good for a moment. Or maybe longer than a moment. You'll find yourself thinking about your everyday tasks with a feeling of positivity and realize you're not focused on your depression anymore. Eventually you will re-engage with everyday life without the quicksand of depression dragging you down. By not fighting it you will have floated to the surface. You will look back at the pit of quicksand and remember you were able to escape it, and you will feel good about yourself for having been able to.

TWO

The Armor of Identity

M any times in therapy clients talk about how they grew
up learning to function in a particular way but that
this way no longer seems to work. They might be experiencing
relationships involving work, love, or family that seem to have
gone stale, gotten stuck, or become stressful and unhappy (or
all of the above). This is often a result of the conflict between
how we learned to act growing up versus how we would like to
act as an adult.

We are born as blank slates. From the moment we pop out
of that warm, cozy womb and cry in shock at the rudeness of
this cold world we start to adapt. We deal with anger, fear,
unhappiness, and trauma by learning how to protect ourselves.
In a perfect world our parents would give us just the right
amount of nurturing, support, and space to grow up and
develop into perfect adults. But the world is far from perfect (as
are our parents!), and it is the scars of our childhood that
shape our present selves. If we have inattentive parents we

might learn to think we don't need that much nurturing. If we have abusive parents we might learn to blame ourselves as the cause of other peoples' anger. If our parents have unrealistic expectations for us we might learn that no matter how hard we try we'll never be good enough. If we experience mental or physical trauma that hurts too much to deal with consciously we might learn to deny or repress bad feelings. There are myriad ways we learn to protect ourselves over the course of our childhood development. These ways are called defense mechanisms, and they are all different variations on the same thing: defending ourselves from feeling we don't want to feel.

We protect ourselves by building a suit of armor. Each piece of this suit is an adaptation, a defense mechanism. Denial, repression, avoidance, rationalization, humor, the list of defense mechanisms is long. Each experience with trauma leads us to fashion a piece of this suit of armor to help protect ourselves from the pain. Some of us might fashion our suit out of only one type of armor. Some of us build a suit that is a collection of different types of armor. We don't do this on purpose. We don't plan on it. We don't even recognize that we're doing it. It's just something we are programmed to do.

And it works! Our psychological development is a fascinating process, the result of millions of years of evolution. When people say things about how the human body is a wonderful, complex machine, remember that it's not just the body, it's the mind as well. If we didn't have this built in process of emotional protection we'd be miserable! We'd constantly be thinking about the unhappiness and disappointment and trauma we have endured in the past, and anticipating that next set of equally negative circumstances sure to come in the future. These defense mechanisms allow us to proceed through life without being overwhelmed by traumas large and small. But there's a downside to this.

As we get older we continue to wear this suit of armor. We grow up, make friends, experience relationships, live our lives. We go through a range of experiences and emotions that we might not necessarily need to protect ourselves from in the same way we did in our childhood. We still wear that same suit of armor that we first started fashioning from the day we were born, all through our childhoods, and we still react to the outside stimulus regarding things that pain us in the same way they did in our childhood. We're wearing a suit of armor that used to be so helpful in protecting ourselves, but now it's part of the problem. It now protects us from things we might not want to be protected against.

The suit of armor that we built to protect us now isolates us, prevents us from acting in ways that might be more appropriate to the situation or relationship. You might reach a point in your life where you feel like you're not yourself. You find yourself in a job, or a relationship, or a life situation that you don't identify with, where you don't recognize the person you've become. That's because as we grow and age we eventually start to identify ourselves less as the true person we are and more as the suit of armor we have built to protect us. After learning to appreciate this metaphor we can take a look in the metaphorical mirror, and instead of our normal self we might see a person hidden behind a complicated suit of armor. Over the years the suit of armor has been assembled so slowly we didn't even recognize we were changing, but now, with this newfound sense of awareness, we see we're wearing a full on suit of armor and we don't recognize ourselves anymore. Somewhere deep down inside that suit of armor is our true self. Over the years our identities have become the accumulations of defenses we have built to protect ourselves, only the problem is we've done it too well.

We are still our authentic selves, of course, but that nugget of personality is deep down in the safe confines of the suit of armor. Now that we are aware of this suit of armor we can start to examine it, to appreciate what we're protecting ourselves from, and if it's still worth protecting. Have we been protecting ourselves from disappointment, but now find ourselves protecting against vulnerability? Have we been defending ourselves from anger, but now find ourselves defending against commitment? Is it time to let down the defenses and let in what we thought were our enemies but now see are really our allies?

Starting with this awareness, and continuing with an examination of our armor, we can begin to remove the pieces one by one and start to feel comfortable as our true selves, ready to experience aspects of life that we once protected ourselves against. So recognize your suit of armor and start to appreciate when you need it and when you don't. You will appreciate relationships much more as you start to realize the armor has been preventing you from being as close and intimate as you imagine a relationship should be. Learn to remove the armor and reveal your true self to the people around you. In this way you will find your authentic self, and begin to live a happier life.

THREE

How to Win (Lose) in a Relationship

In therapy it's common to hear people in relationships talk about their interactions with their partners in terms of "keeping score". This is the idea that we consider perceived slights or the neglect of our emotional needs as attacks against us, as if an opponent is scoring points against us in a game. Our instinct is to respond to these perceived attacks with our own counter attacks in an effort to even the score. Thinking about it objectively, we can see that this idea of keeping score isn't going to help our relationship. In fact, we know that if we want a happy relationship we should refrain from playing the game, because if we win, it means our partner loses. However, in the heat of the moment, keeping score feels completely justified and indeed the right thing to do. It can be very satisfying to let our partner know in ways both straightforward and indirect that we are right and they are wrong. That we can hurt them more than they hurt us. We do this in many ways, from big things like pointing out in an unsupportive way how a career change hasn't worked out for the best, to small things like pointing out a better parking spot that could have been had. And we often do it without acknowledging we are doing it. This deeply seated need to keep score keeps us from having relationships as supportive and meaningful as they could be.

When we have a solid relationship base, and feel like a united front against the trials and tribulations of life, we often think about ourselves as members of the same team. We're in the trenches together, we've got each other's back. But when we keep score we're not on the same team anymore. Now we're opponents. We're turning our relationship into a competition where one person is always losing. And how do we ultimately win in this particular game? We make the other person so aware of what they are doing wrong and how they are failing us in our relationship that we reach the point where they no longer want to be around us. The end goal of the game is to be so right that it eventually drives the other person away. And most importantly, it should happen in a way that makes it feel like it's not our fault. That the other person made this happen. They made the choice to leave. Of course, the reason why is because we played the game so well. That's the horrible irony of this game: By winning it we ultimately lose.

It can be very difficult to break out of this mindset. To stop looking at the scoreboard. To not even care what the score is. To not feel like a pushover who doesn't mind losing. To stop living in the mindset of competition at all. Of course, to get to this point you have to accept that you are playing the game in the first place. Most people never even get to the point where they realize this. They go from relationship to relationship, always winning the game but losing the war. So, the first step is awareness. The next step is to learn how to not play.

Imagine you're a basketball player in a close game. You have the ball with a chance to take the lead with a last second shot. It's your time in the spotlight, your moment to shine. But instead, as the clock counts down, you simply hand the ball to an opposing player. The buzzer sounds, you've lost the game. The fans are furious. You didn't even take a shot! The way those fans would react is how your subconscious mind will react when your partner says something you take to be an attack on yourself, something that makes you feel ashamed or defensive, and you don't come back with an equally mean reply. When you defer the choice about where to eat dinner to them and then you go to the place and it's closed and you don't take the opportunity to needle them about it. When you accept what your emotional self considers to be an attack on yourself without retaliating. When you don't take the shot. The voices in your head will yell and boo and demand you take that shot, but now you know that it's not about winning the game. In fact, it's not a game at all! The opponent you thought you were playing against is actually your teammate.

It's hard to break this pattern, and like most things that are hard to do, it starts with small steps. Eventual change stems from the realization that we don't have to point out when our partners do something wrong. That what you perceive to be an attack on you is not an attack at all. And in small moments we can think about this and react in ways that are not defensive. We can let moments like this pass without reacting to them. You will be pleasantly surprised by how much these incremental changes in your attitude will improve your relationship.

Little things mean a lot. When situations that once were sure to turn into fights now pass by without conflict that's an improvement. So, learn to lose the game and win the war. Because, in the words of a famous 20th century supercomputer, "The only winning move is not to play".

FOUR

The Metal Detector

One of the aspects of mental health we focus on in talk therapy is how we think. We each have a way of thinking about ourselves that is established at an early age and has become so ingrained in us that we don't recognize how much it affects our lives. Therapeutic modalities like Cognitive Behavior Therapy (CBT) can help us reframe the way we think and allow us to feel differently about things. Our thoughts influence, affect, and can even control our feelings. This concept is expressed through a parable about a metal detector.

Once upon a time there was a person who lived by the beach, and every day they walked up and down with a metal detector, looking for treasure. This person was determined, lugging the metal detector up and down the beach all day long. Unfortunately, this person never found any treasure. They only found trash. Plastic bags, bottles and cans, cheap broken watches, empty wallets, lone flip flops, broken sunglasses, all the kinds of trash one could possibly find at the beach.

This person was disappointed and frustrated, but never gave up. Even though they only found trash they continued to show up every day. Other people came and went, spending time at the beach without looking for buried treasure. Some came in the morning, some in the afternoon, some in the evening, all enjoying the time they spent there according to their own personal preferences. Some of them noticed the person with the metal detector, but most of them paid them no mind.

One day this person got so frustrated with only finding trash that they gave up and started to cry. It started slowly at first, but then grew in intensity. It was an intense release of emotions, and after a few minutes of this, the crying gave way to anger, and the person yelled in frustration, throwing the metal detector down and giving it a kick. After this outburst the person felt better, and picked up the metal detector again, ready to continue the search. That's when they noticed something on the the control panel: It had been set to the "find trash" setting. So this person adjusted the dial instead to the "find treasure" setting, and then started to walk up and down the beach again.

This time the results were different. This person began to find treasure. A gold ring, a silver necklace, a fancy watch, a wallet. There weren't as many treasures as trash, but the person was thrilled to finally find something good. Something positive. It was as if all the bad times finding only trash had never even happened. Life was good. They had finally figured out out how to be happy!

The next day the person came to the beach again, excited to find more treasure, but right off the bat found only trash. This person grew more and more frustrated as the day went on. They didn't notice that the dial on the metal detector had gotten turned back to the trash setting. However, they never thought about checking the control panel. They had completely forgotten about it. It was as if the big discovery from the day before had never happened. They just resumed walking up and down the beach, finding nothing but trash, and stewing in the familiar frustration.

Towards the end of the day there was a beautiful sunset. The people at the beach all took notice and enjoyed it, but our person was so frustrated after another day of finding only trash they didn't notice the beautiful sunset. They were completely focused on how depressed and disappointed they felt. They sat down on a bench, feeling as lonely and hopeless as ever. That's when one of the beachgoers walked over and asked about the control panel on the metal detector. The person's eyes lit up as they remembered what had happened the previous day, and as they turned the dial back to the treasure setting they immediately felt better, like a weight was lifted off their shoulders. Then they looked up and noticed the sunset, and also noticed the people around them watching the sunset as well. So instead of going out to search for treasure, our person sat on the bench with the helpful beachgoer, watching the sunset, enjoying the moment.

As the sun continued to set, our treasure hunting person vowed to always remember to check and make sure the metal detector was set to detect treasure. If they could just remember to do that, life would be so easy! And so, in the future, this person kept coming back to the beach every day, sometimes finding trash, and sometimes finding treasure. Sometimes after a long streak of finding only trash the person would remember to check the settings on the metal detector, turn the dial back to the correct setting, and then go on a streak of finding treasure. In this way, the person lived the rest of their life happier than they had been before.

What do the figures in this parable represent? The metal detector represents your mind, and the treasure and the trash are good and bad feelings. Some peoples' minds seem set to only focus on the negatives, to always find the bad thoughts and feelings (trash) about any situation. Their minds are stuck on the trash setting just like the metal detector, focusing on the negative, ignoring the positive feelings, the things in life to be proud of and feel good about (treasure).

That friendly beachgoer who pointed out to the person that the dial had flipped back to the trash setting? That person is a therapist. Or a friend. Or a family member. Anyone close enough to the person to point out the good things in their life. Who can dig deeper and ask questions about why we're feeling what we're feeling. Someone who can pull the person out of their tunnel vision point of view, so focused on the negative, and remind them of the treasure all around them.

Some people don't have this problem, this self-defeating focus on negativity. For whatever reason, they can go through life not only without finding any trash, but without spending any time looking for it. They don't even have a metal detector! For them, the treasure (good feelings) is all around them, easily found and enjoyed, just like a sunset at the beach. For those of us that focus on the negative, these people seem "normal" to us, which makes us feel less-than-normal, separate, different. But in those moments when we can allow ourselves to look up and notice the sunset, we feel like one of the crowd, like a member of the group, like we're "normal".

Some people go through life with their metal detectors always set on trash. They're unable to see the treasure. Sometime they're so invested in this process that when other people point out that their metal detector is on the wrong setting they refuse to acknowledge it. You are not like this, however. You know that you have the power to turn your dial to the desired setting and notice the treasure all around you. And even when you're finding only trash, you still know the treasure is out there, waiting to be found. Your life is like the beach in this story. It's a beautiful place meant to be enjoyed, but you must give yourself the freedom to do so. Remember to make sure your emotional metal detector is on the right setting!

FIVE

Our Changing Normals

P eople often come to talk therapy for help dealing with a major change in their lives. In fact, I would say dealing with change is one of the most common situations that create issues for people to address in therapy. It could be a change in a relationship, a change within their family, or a change regarding work. It could be caused by something internal and specific to the client, or it could be something external and universal. The clients I see have much in common regarding the cause of the changes in their lives, as many of them have to do with a situation created by the pandemic in some way. Changes like these can be harder to process than most of the relatively smaller changes we experience in our lives. By process, I mean the work of learning to acknowledge and accept these changes. Once we can acknowledge and accept that change has come, and that our "normal" life has permanently changed, we can get on with the work of trying to be happy in the moment.

Major changes can happen (or feel like they've happened) in an instant, even if they took years to slowly build up to that point. Big changes like divorce, death, breakups, breakdowns, these kind of changes create a before and an after in our lives. It often seems like we spend more time processing the aftermath of these changes than the events of the change themselves. During this period of time we are likely to experience the processing of this change as anxiety or depression, to feel the struggle to wrap our heads around the events of the past affecting us emotionally and physically in the present. We might feel restless or uncomfortable, like something is nagging at us, not allowing us to be at peace. We yearn to feel safe. And the idea of things being normal is safe. Normal, by definition, is the opposite of change. And if things are safe now, and they don't change, then we're safe. So, we strive for normal. But what is normal?

Normal is, in this context, the past. Normal is the safety of knowing how things turn out. It feels good striving for a return to a sense of normalcy because we sometimes feel better thinking about the past than we do the present, where the future is uncertain. I think what makes it hard for us to enjoy happiness in the moment is our tendency to hold on too tightly to happiness from the past. When we idealize the past and subconsciously crave a return to that safer, more certain time, we are taking energy and focus away from being in the present, which is ultimately where we spend our lives.

A phrase that comes up in session with clients regarding this process is "let go to grow". It refers to our tendency to hold on to the past to the detriment of our future. It often applies to situations where the client feels stuck or at a dead end in life, love, or career. We often find that the things holding us back from changing our lives for the better are not the events that might happen to us so much as the events that have happened to us. Meaning, we are ruled by our reactions and expectations to future possibilities that are based on events from much earlier in our lives.

How do we let go to grow? This is the work of talk therapy. We talk about what we're holding on to and why. What feels good about it, what we don't like about it. We take stock of where we are now after removing the filter of our expectations from the past. We identify the new normals that might be available to us after periods of change. We identify when we're comparing our present experience to our past expectations, and learn to let go of them. Our present becomes the new normal.

Our experience in the post pandemic business environment is reflective of this personal emotional state. The businesses that succeed seem to be the ones that adapt and incorporate lessons learned during the pandemic into their future operations. The ones that base their future expectations based on how business was before March 2020 are going to be disappointed with how things are in the future, since things will never go back to being like there were back then. Likewise, people who expect their emotional lives to go back to normal are going to be disappointed as well. As with any major life change, the event that occurs to affect the change is just one part of it. It's the change that occurs within ourselves that affects our lives the most. How we interpret or react to the objective event that causes the change. Happier people seem to be able to adapt to the changing normals more easily. People who constantly talk about how things used to be before everything changed don't seem very happy to me. Let's work on spending less time waiting for things get back to normal to be happy, and more time finding reasons to be happy right now.

There's a Reason We Cliché

A cliché is a phrase or opinion that feels overused and lacking in original thought. We call something a cliché when we've heard it a million times, so often that any meaning it once had has been eclipsed by our collective shrug when we hear it again. We sometimes experience negative thoughts about ourselves when we use these clichés, because it implies we are lacking in original thought. And for some reason, to be lacking in original thought is a bad thing. We should suffer in original ways!

In talk therapy this experience often plays out as a client starts to become more aware of their own patterns of behavior. Let's say I have been working with a client for a few months, and we've established a process for dealing with an issue (how they interact with their partner, how they resolve conflict with their children, their relationship with their parents, etc). We'll discuss the interaction, with the client commenting on what they were feeling at the time, and what they think about it now. At some point, as they come to an understanding of their issues in a new way, they might use a common phrase that applies to the situation they find themselves in. Some saying that encapsulates what they are trying to say with the minimum amount of words necessary. Something that makes them laugh and shrug as they say it. They use a cliché.

It's a Process. It's Not About Me. I Have the Power to Say No. I Have To Learn To Love Myself Before Someone Else Can Love Me. It Is What It Is. Pick a cliché. They seem trite as listed here, but in everyone's life there are serious times of contemplation and realization where a cliché like these makes perfect sense. Clichés simplify things. They make a complicated situation feel more manageable. They make sense.

As clients observe themselves using these clichés they often shake their heads and grin, chuckling to themselves about how much of a cliché they must sound like. Here we have a conversation about what a cliché actually is. The first guy who said The Sun Will Come Out Tomorrow must have sounded like a genius. The millionth guy got told to shut up. It Takes Two to Tango? Yeah, yeah. It's Always Darkest Before the Dawn? Gimme a break. The Best is Yet To Come? Shut up. However, the original meaning of these phrases, the messages of hope, optimism, the power of faith, those still apply. These themes can create positive feelings to remember in dark days, when you're at your lowest. The reason these sound like clichés is that they are all so simply and undeniably true.

Here we need to realize that we don't necessarily have to feel bad about engaging in a cliché. Let's give ourselves permission to not be original. If you find yourself using clichés more often, it's probably because you've reduced your inner conflict down to a manageable level where the cliché is a shortcut through all the work you've done to remind yourself that Only Time Will Tell, Time Heals All Wounds, and There's No Time Like the Present. Or, you might be putting off dealing with all that inner conflict by focussing on something a lot simpler so you don't have to deal with the bigger issues, like how This Too Shall Pass, Better Late Than Never, or The Grass Is Greener on the Other Side. Either way, consider feeling good about using clichés. They are a sign you're on the right path.

SEVEN

It's Not Just a Joke

I n therapy sessions the topics of conversation are often pretty serious. There is usually a significant amount of tension involved. A common instinct in many people when they feel tension is to undercut it with humor. Making a joke about a serious topic releases the tension and makes us feel more comfortable. Humor is also a way to say what you really feel without having to completely commit to it. Jokes are an important arrow in the conversational quiver for people who are passive aggressive. They are a way to say how you feel without admitting how you feel. After all, it's just a joke, right?

It's never just a joke. Okay fine, sometimes it is just a joke. But there is always a nugget of truth inside the joke. It's like how we give dogs pills by putting them inside a scoop of peanut butter. The pills are the truth, and the peanut butter is the humor that makes it go down easier. Or unnoticed. For most of my life I made a living making jokes. In a professional setting, writing comedy for film and television, my job was to understand the personalities of the characters in the shows I wrote for, the type of family life they experienced growing up that molded them into the people they have become, all the factors of their personality that would influence their point of view and how they would express it, and write jokes from that point of view. It is through a strong understanding of a character's psychological makeup that the basis for their jokes is discovered. That's what makes a great joke, in my opinion. It's funny, but it also reflects a characters' personality and point of view. As viewers, this is how we appreciate a good joke. It's the point of view motivating the character making the joke.

However, that's the world according to television comedy, which, while approximating reality, is far different from it. Similar jokes made between romantic partners, parents, or co-workers in real life often do not land as well. These are the jokes that don't have the luxury of a laugh track to soften the blow. Sometimes these jokes are ways for us to express emotions like anger, fear, jealousy, or shame, but in a safer way than talking about them openly. These are the jokes that are so clearly manifestations of the uncomfortable truth that we feel obligated to say "It's just a joke!".

A therapy session is a different ballgame, though. Here we do not have to end on a laugh. The tension here is not to be cut; it is to be embraced. In my work as a comedy writer, the goal was to find humor in these tense moments. In my work as a therapist, the goal is to find the truth in these moments. The last thing I want to do when a client says something emotionally significant and wrought with deeper meaning is to undercut it with a joke. And when the client makes a joke revealing something emotionally significant with deeper mean-

EIGHT

The Stinky Cheese Smell of Shame

S hame lies at the heart of many of the issues that bring people to therapy. The dictionary definition of shame is "a painful feeling of humiliation or distress caused by the consciousness of wrong or foolish behavior." Shame is something that can be so ingrained in our lives from an early age that we don't appreciate how powerfully it affects us in the present. It can become an essential part of our personality, completely hidden but guiding our lives, until we recognize it and start to talk about it.

Shame is different than guilt. Guilt is the feeling we get when we do something bad, something we know is wrong. It's something we can fix by doing better next time. We can give ourselves another chance. Shame is much more diabolical. Shame makes us feel not that we did something bad, but that we _are_ something bad. Instead of feeling like we did something wrong, we feel like we _are_ something wrong. Shame is like a little piece of cheese hidden deep down inside us in a crevice that is difficult to find and hard to reach. It fell into a crack in our psyche at an early age, and over the years it started to go bad and stink. Maybe when we were children we were exposed to anger, made to feel worthless, powerless, that instead of doing things that were wrong we were in fact wrong ourselves. Things as simple as spilling a glass of milk at the dinner table that, depending on the parents' or caregivers' reaction, can go from making us feel like we did something wrong, to that we are a bad child who can do nothing right and there is inherently something wrong with us which is proved by events such as this. Shame starts early!

Each experience like this is like hiding little pieces of stinky cheese deep in the consciousness of our true selves. The cheese of shame is always there, slowly rotting, and smelling worse and worse over time. The irony is, even though this shame smell is so powerful, by the time we become adults we're used to it. We've lived with it so long we don't even notice the smell anymore. But unconsciously, we're completely aware of it. Deep down we know we stink, and we act like we know we stink, and we expect other people in our lives to smell this stink and wrinkle their noses at us. To think we are bad. To think we stink. For shame!

But here's the thing: Other people can't smell our cheese! It's not even on their radar. They can, however, sense that we smell the cheese. They see us act in ways that make it clear we think we stink. The way we protect or demean ourselves, the attitude we have about ourselves, our inability to express our vulnerability or provide emotional support for our partners, these are all manifestations of us being guided by the stinky cheese smell of shame. People around us, friends, family, loved ones, they don't smell the cheese anymore. In fact, we might do such a good job searching for the cheese, examining the cheese, talking about the cheese, we might emotionally clean the cheese smell out completely. But the truth is, the smell will always linger in our memories. We have lived with that cheese for so long, building walls around it, hiding from it, feeling bad about it, so the smell will always exist in our minds.

In working with clients on this issue, I try to find situations where the smell of shame might have guided them towards conflict and tension and anxiety in the past. Times when we feel like we stink, and that other people can smell this, and that other people will know we stink and think less of us, that people in our lives that we love will think we are bad people because we smell. We explore the shameful feelings, and through that process we are able to find the metaphorical cheese and clean it up, to get rid of the stinky crumbs. We use lavender scented cleaning products and a nice damp sponge and end up with a sparkling inner fridge.

But just because we've found the stinky cheese and cleaned it doesn't mean we're free of it. That smell was with us a long time, and the feelings it caused will always be with us. The goal of therapy is to become aware of these feelings and learn to accept them but not let them dictate our lives. We can't get rid of shame, but we can understand it, accept it, and not let it define us. We can remind ourselves that even though the cheese is gone, the smell stays with us. But look at the people around you. They don't look like they just got a whiff of stinky cheese. They aren't wrinkling their noses at you. They only smell your lavender scented cleaning product. But we'll always remember the smell of the stinky cheese, even after we eliminate its power to influence our lives.

NINE

The Personal Growth Two Step

I t can be frustrating to measure the progress of personal growth that is a result of talk therapy. This change is often slow and incremental, and we want results now. Especially after we've spent a good amount of time working to identify the issues about ourselves we want to address. That in and of itself is a victory. To be able to identify specific issues about yourself you want to change is a win. It can often feel like you've been on a long hike, climbing a steep hill, and you're looking forward to cresting the hill and seeing your final destination laid out in from of you. However, what often happens is you make the difficult climb, get to the top of the hill, and look over the other side only to see another hill for you to climb. Life, am I right?

This feeling isn't restricted only to the beginning stages of talk therapy. It's something that occurs throughout the process, and throughout life. We feel like we are doing the work we need to do to get us to the finish line and finally get to start enjoying life as our new and improved selves, but eventually see that there is no finish line, and that the journey, the ups and downs, the progression and regression, the work, this is how life really plays out. This frustration is often expressed by clients as a feeling that for every two steps forward they take, they take one step back. This is said with such a negative connotation that I sometimes have to double check what was said. Was it *one* step forward and *two* steps back? Because that would certainly be depressing. That would mean that no progress would ever be made. We'd be moving backwards. That I could see as being truly disheartening.

However, when we say two steps forward, one step back, we're making progress. We're moving forwards! Perhaps the frustrating thing is that we expect personal growth to happen in a straightforward way. We don't always appreciate the two steps forward part of it because we're too busy thinking about the one step back we just took. So, if you find yourself feeling discouraged with the back and forth nature of personal growth, try to continue to appreciate the two steps forward part, but let's rethink the one step back aspect. Instead of a step back, let's think of it as a break. A pause. A moment to stop and reflect on our path, the progress we've made, and what's impeding that progress. Instead of feeling like that we are not progressing in this moment, let's think about it as a chance to recharge and prepare for our next two steps forward. And consider this: The nature of the personal growth and change we seek requires that we take a step back every now and then. That we encounter difficulty. That we struggle. That we doubt. That we fail. And it is through this failure that we learn how to change. In fact, it might be that it is this failure that forces us to change. When we protect ourselves from failure, when we simply do not try to change, then we remain stuck.

Two steps forward, one step back is not a negative situation. It's the natural progression of things. That one step back can be anticipated when things are going well, and just as importantly those two steps forward can be anticipated when things are not going well. When I'm working with clients who voice this two step phenomenon in a negative way, we work on reframing it into something positive, a sign of progress. Then, after that next instance of two more steps of progress and one step back, we are able to appreciate this as a sign of growth and feel good about it, as opposed to a sign of failure that we should feel bad about. Two steps forward and one step back will eventually win the race! We just have to accept that it's going to take a bit longer than we thought.

TEN

Dude, Where's My Car-tharsis?

M ost people don't know that when writing the early drafts of "Dude, Where's My Car?" I was heavily influenced by post-Kantian philosophers like Hegel and Schopenhauer. In fact, the first completed version of the script wouldn't even be considered a comedy. It was originally more of a "Waiting for Godot" type philosophical back and forth between two characters questioning their place in the universe. Only after getting lost deep in the existential considerations regarding human consciousness and the meaning of life did I finally decide to go with the lighter, funnier version that eventually got made. In fact, the movie's original title was "Dude, What is the Meaning of Life?" In this chapter, we're going to explore how the story of the film can be considered a metaphor to help understand the story of life.

So, two dudes spend the movie looking for their car, stumbling between comedy scenes, trying to order Chinese food, finding tattoos on their backs, and encountering a gang of people wearing bubble wrap jump suits. Most people who talk to me about the movie tend to point out which scene was their favorite. Where they laughed the hardest. What line of dialogue was the most memorable. What nobody has ever said to me is "I liked the movie, but while I was watching it I found that I couldn't enjoy it because the whole time I was thinking about when they were going to find the car."

That's because the point of the movie isn't finding the car. The point of the movie is what happens during the journey to find the car. It's the manifestation of that classic saying, "Life is the journey, not the destination". I've heard this truism my whole life. I'm sure you have too. But many times we don't really comprehend sayings like this until we experience moments that force us to embrace the deeper meaning behind them.

The idea of catharsis, meaning the process of releasing and thus providing relief from strong or repressed emotions, is central to talk therapy. Clients often seek therapy because of the effect of strong repressed emotions that cause or are affected by traumatic events in their lives. One goal of therapy is to uncover these strong emotions and let them out. The problems they cause might not be solved immediately, but clients often experience a great sense of relief after a realization like this has been achieved. In therapy sessions this concept of experiencing catharsis seems to always be present to some degree, from being actively explored to lying just below the surface. Therapy is very much about identifying, accepting, and releasing the strong emotions that guide our lives with an often times invisible hand.

Many people want to avoid situations that force them to

embrace the kind of powerful emotions that get repressed. It's our natural reaction, our default setting. Repression is one of the most common defense mechanisms we develop to protect ourselves from emotional and physical trauma. Put simply, we don't want to think about things that make us feel bad. But these moments of catharsis find us no matter how much we try to avoid them, and often this happens towards the ends of our lives, just as it does towards the ends of movies. In movies this makes sense, because it wraps up the movie and then we leave the theater with whatever lessons we've learned and continue on with our lives. In real life this is less desirable. Why wait till the end of your life to experience something that could improve the quality of your life? The lesson here is, don't spend your whole life running from hard moments that could lead to catharsis.

How else to apply the spiritual lessons of this cinematic classic to our lives? We can feel inspired to live in the moment, to recognize ourselves in the present and not be overly concerned with what will happen in the future or what went on in the past. Let your life be about enjoying the search for your own metaphorical car. The one certainty in life is that we will all eventually find our cars, and if you've been thinking about finding the car your whole life you will be under-whelmed at the end of the movie. You certainly don't want to find your metaphorical car and then realize you wish you'd spent less time thinking about finding it and more time enjoying the time spent searching for it.

So after you finish this chapter close the book, take a moment and think about what makes you feel good in this moment, at this time in your life, at this point in your journey, during this scene in your own bio-pic. Focus on this moment and let yourself enjoy it without worrying about what is to come. Don't consider the choices you could have made in the past that might have led you to a different place in the present. Consider where you are right now your destination, and give yourself credit for reaching it. Because, as a wise man named Gautama Buddha once said, "You will find your happiness in the searching for the car, not in the finding of it".

ELEVEN

The Ticking Clock of Meditation

Mindfulness refers to the feeling of a moment by moment awareness of our thoughts, physical sensations, and environment. It's a practice that can help us learn to regulate emotions and decrease stress and anxiety. It's a state of mind. When you're mindful, you're not "stuck in your head" or "lost in your thoughts". You're focused on the moment at hand, without all the chatter and concern for the future or the past. Clients who are interested in using mindfulness to help deal with stress and anxiety often start with meditation. It's the most familiar of the mindfulness practices. Learning to meditate is not easy, although it seems like it should be. You're just sitting there doing nothing, right? It makes sense, but once we try to meditate we realize it's not that easy to do nothing. The pace of modern life, with all its responsibilities and expectations, as well as our own evolutionary-shaped brains trained to analyze past experiences and anticipate future ones, are in direct opposition to the concept of meditation. I find that the more overwhelmed I feel by my to-do list, the more I feel recharged by the experience of a good meditation session. It can be a wonderful practice once you find a way to do it that suits you.

There are a variety of styles of meditation. There's mindfulness meditation, progressive relaxation, Transcendental Meditation, Kundalini yoga, Zen meditation, and many others. There are also apps like Headspace and Insight Timer that can provide a framework that is user-friendly and takes advantage of technology to facilitate the experience. The reality is that there are as many ways to meditate as there are people who meditate. This can make it difficult when you're starting out, trying to find an entry point among so many choices to start your own meditation practice. It took me a long time to develop the style that suits me best. Much of that time was spent trying different practices, not enjoying them, and then feeling like I was failing to do them correctly, and then feeling bad about that. If this is similar to your experience, I would encourage you to keep trying, keep experimenting, until you find a way that works for you. That's what I did.

When I meditate, my goal is to be in the moment. Meaning, to be aware of the environment around me. More specifically, my goal is to <u>not</u> think about the past or the future. Things like what I'm going to cook for dinner, whether I should have chosen a different major in college, or how much my estimated taxes for the second quarter are going to be. I like to imagine these thoughts as pebbles tossed into the pool of my mind, and the goal is to stop tossing those pebbles. One of the ways I do this is by hearing the ticking clock.

I sit on my couch in my living room when I meditate. As I

start my session I can hear the birds outside chirping and the low hum of traffic passing on the street. I focus on these sounds, breathing slowly and deeply through my nose. There is some back and forth between my mind and my thoughts, as my mind tries to focus on the moment while my thoughts race around trying to distract me. Then I hear something that's always there but I hardly ever notice: the ticking of the clock hanging on the wall.

It's your standard black and white IKEA clock. When I notice the ticking sound I'm always a little surprised. This is a sound that happens every second of every day, at the same volume, a volume at which I can clearly hear in the moment. Yet during the rest of my day I don't hear it. Most of the time it's because there are other sounds that drown it out. Sometimes it's because the thoughts in my head drown it out. But it's always there, whether I hear it or not. This ticking sound represents the moment. And most of the time, my mind is too busy thinking about other things to notice it. But by focusing on the ticking sound during meditation, I find myself in the present. I'm not thinking about what happened in the past, or what might happen in the future. I'm focused on being here right now, and the ticking clock reminds me of this.

And then of course my mind starts to wander, and I find myself thinking about what groceries I need or how much I don't like my new hair cut or something my mom said last week that annoyed me and then led to feelings of guilt for being annoyed at my mom. And then I realize my mind has wandered, so I refocus, take a deep breath, and listen for the ticking clock again. By repeating this process of being aware of the moment, feeling at peace about it, then feeling my thoughts run away and refocusing again, I'm learning to train my brain to be less obsessed about thoughts of the past and the future. It gets quieter inside my mind.

This approach to meditation is what works for me. You should feel free to try it without feeling like it has to work for you. I encourage you to read books on meditation, search for information about it, be curious about how other people approach it, how they meditate, and then take what you like from each to build your own practice. If it's something you enjoy, keep at it. If you don't enjoy it, try something else. Do it your own way. Find your own ticking clock!

TWELVE

Zoom Out

When a client comes to see me, often times they are in crisis. They have been experiencing anxiety, depression, fear, anger, or any number of emotions that have made their lives unhappy to the point where they have decided that they need help, and now they're willing to take the steps they need to take to get that help. There might have been a recent traumatic experience like a break up or a death, or they might be feeling the effects of a long term issue like chronic anxiety or depression. Either way, our process is similar. We start out talking about how that client's particular issue affects them in their everyday lives. A story about a fight with their spouse, or a panic attack, or a bout of depression leaving them unable to work, something that represents the cycle of unhappiness they are experiencing. Then we delve into the causes of this cycle, both the immediate, practical factors, as well as the more personal, emotional factors. At first it's hard for the client to think objectively about something so emotionally intense.

They often feel that when they're in the middle of these strong emotions, it's like they're on a raft going down a raging river, water spraying in their face, close to capsizing, holding on for dear life. This is what it feels like when we're in the thrall of intense emotions. Sitting with me talking about it in session, they are often able to experience some distance from these emotions, and observe the process as if they were on the bank of the imaginary river, watching themselves go down the rapids.

This is a key step in learning to process the emotions that have been guiding us to an unhappy place. When we're experiencing these emotional cycles, when we're truly "in it", we can feel like we're at the mercy of powers stronger than ourselves, powerless to change things, like a wind up toy moving along with no choice in the matter. When we are able to get some distance from these events and analyze our feelings and actions in a more objective way, we start to gain some awareness. I call this Zooming Out. It's the whole point of talk therapy, in a way; discussing an emotional event that happened without being under the control of the emotions that caused it, enabling us to learn more about it in a way that might empower us to change how we react the next time it happens.

After developing the ability to discuss what it was like being powerless in the face of strong emotions, eventually the client gets to the point where, the next time something like this happens in their everyday life, they are able to Zoom Out in the moment. They feel themselves being tossed around by the raging river of their emotions, but are able to step back and imaging themselves standing on the bank of the river, watching themselves struggling on the raft, surrounded by white water, hanging on for dear life. I've had clients describe this as sort of an out of body experience, to see themselves in the throes of anxiety or depression or relationship conflict or work stress, and at the same time to be able to stand beside themselves and observe this happening with a calmer, observant disposition. As this process of Zooming Out continues, the client is able to report on how they saw themselves acting, why they were doing the things they were doing, and how they are able to recognize the pattern they were stuck in.

At first the client feels powerless to change things. Even though they have this newfound sense of awareness, they are unable to do anything to change the cycle they are experiencing. But eventually, through the process of talk therapy, they are able to go from Zooming Out to Zooming Back In. This is when they are able to do something in the moment to break out of the negative cycle. It's as if they are on the raging river, deep in the rapids, but now have an oar they are able to use to paddle to safety. The feeling of powerlessness is eventually replaced by a sense that we can indeed do something to change the situation. The aware part of ourselves slowly gains control of our actions from the unaware part of ourselves. This is often a breakthrough moment for clients, the moment when they realize they are doing something they don't want to do, feeling some way they don't want to feel, and finally feeling like they are able to do something about it.

Now, what can they do about it? Not much, at first. Often just being aware of it is the start. But soon they are able to ask themselves questions that can lead to a different approach to the situation. Why am I getting so angry about this? Why am I taking out my anger on this person? Is the way I'm acting helping me live a happier life? Do I have the power to not act this way? These are all questions that will lead us to a better awareness of what has brought us to this point, and what we can do to change our lives for the better. Zooming Out is the technique we use here, with the idea that eventually we will take the skills we learned on the outside and then Zoom Back In and apply them in order to change things for the better.

THIRTEEN

The Mind Makes Bad Movies

W e all have an inner critic. The part of ourselves that disapproves of and criticizes the things we think, say, and do. In some of us that critic has a disproportionally large influence on how we feel about ourselves. This inner critic conjures up images of how we might fail in the future, all the things that can go wrong, and how bad we're going to feel if we try things and fail, because all we've done is fail in the past anyways. Our imagination creates scenarios that reinforce our belief that we're going to (or already have) screwed things up. It's like the inner critic hijacks our imagination to make bad movies that we are forced to watch.

These movies are not feel good movies. We might have pleasant daydreams, but for many of us, the films running in our minds are not sunny and positive. Most often they're scary or sad movies, full of fears about the future and regrets about the past. They are somber dramas examining the many ways the star of the movie (ourselves) has screwed things up in life.

Classic feel-bad movies, the kind you would never want to see in a theater, are for some reason the most popular at the box office of our minds. And there's no lack of ideas for these movies. There's an inexhaustible supply of fears and anxiety to develop into scripts. They have titles like "Fears That My Fiancé is Having Second Thoughts", "Stupid Things You Said at the Holiday Party", and "You're Going to Die Alone III: Valentine's Day".

Why do our minds produce such bad movies? I think there's a deep seated evolutionary reason for this. When our cave man ancestors existed many years ago, struggling to find shelter and food, they had to worry about all the bad things that might happen because it gave them more of a chance to avoid these things. They had to consider every animal that could be out there waiting to eat them, every journey to find food that could end in disaster. These movies had titles like "When Animals Attack Our Tribe", "Caught in a Storm Without Shelter", and "Left Behind II: Broken Ankle". Our caveman ancestors had to consider the possibility of these situations in order to be ready for them. The ones who didn't weren't prepared when something bad happened, and they were the ones who got eaten or starved to death. Nature weeded out the cavemen who didn't think about the worst case scenarios. The ones that were left were the ones who thought about the most horrible situations just in case they happened, and thus were prepared for them when they did. Over the many years from then up until today the mind as movie maker developed its production skills. As our brains grew we developed better tools and nicer production facilities. As civilization grew and culture developed, more and more material became available for mental filmmaking. Technology provided more fodder for anxiety. The question now is, do these feel bad films still serve a purpose?

I think they do. It's still valuable for us to think about things that could go wrong in the future. Clearly it's in our nature to consider these outcomes. It can be practical at a basic level. But the bigger problem is when the films stop being practical and start being self-destructive, when we can't turn this mind movie making machine off. It gets to the point where these movies only exist only as kindling for the fire of our fears, creating anxiety and depression in a runaway loop that can become box office smashes that dominate our lives. These runaway box office hits with titles like "Unhappy Marriage", "Stuck in a Dead End Career", and "Depression II: Smoking More Weed" dominate the production pipeline. How can we change the tone of these movies? How can we fire the executives who are in charge of developing these feel-bad hits?

When our minds are screening these movies, it's hard to remember that we have the power to get up and walk out of that theater. In real life, even if a movie's bad, we paid for it, and most of the time we don't really want to get up and leave. What if we had the power to change the movie, though? Wouldn't we benefit more from seeing films with titles like "Feeling Pretty Good Today", "Relaxing Family Holiday Visit", and "Relationship II: We Worked It Out."

In talk therapy there are various approaches to this situation. Meditation and mindfulness practices can help us develop the power to turn the channel on these movies, to get up and walk out of the theater and demand a refund. Clinical techniques like cognitive behavioral therapy (CBT) can give us the tools to stop these films before they get produced, and enable us to change the endings from sad to happy. Our mind produces these movies, and on a surface level we know they're not real, that we're just imagining things. On a deeper level of consciousness, though, our brains accept these movies as the truth. That the bad things we are seeing in this film are actually happening. And this can cause our bodies to react as if they are. This stress and anxiety makes us react physically as if we have actually experienced the things we see in these films. Think about this next time you find yourself watching a bad movie in your mind. Remind yourself that it's just your thoughts, it's not reality. Even if you already know this remind yourself. You can choose to see a different movie. Remember, you have the power to get up and walk out of the theater!

FOURTEEN

Just Say No (and then Why)

Many clients self identify as being passive aggressive. For some people, this means they understand how conflict in their relationships exists because of the tension caused by their tendency to express anger indirectly, which was created by their formative childhood experiences. For other people, this just means they get in lots of fights with their partners. My understanding of passive aggressive behavior has to do with a person's inability to freely express anger as a child, and the resulting expression of that anger in less direct ways that avoid confrontation, but still make that anger felt. This often results in the client being passive aggressively angry towards their partner while their partner has no clue about the real reason for this anger.

This played out in my work with a client who was well aware of his passive aggressive tendencies. We had talked about the origins of these feelings, which involved a parent who was full of rage, and would overpower any display of anger on the client's part with his own full force of anger. This made it unsafe for the client to express anger as a child, so he learned to go along but make his anger felt in indirect ways, including sarcasm, humor, irritability, and withdrawal. Now, in his adult relationship with his partner, he could see how acting in the same way as he did growing up is causing conflict and unhappiness.

A common situation where this dynamic played out was when this client's partner asked him to do something he didn't want to do. In session he would describe a fight he and his partner had over something involving cooking dinner, or going on a trip, and we would analyze the situation, the conflict, his approach and feelings at the time. After some time working together, we realized that almost all of these fights started with the client agreeing to do something he didn't want to do. Maybe it was something big, like the decision about where to go on a trip, or something smaller, like not wanting to cook the fish a particular way. So, we had a starting point to focus on.

The question became: Why did this client say yes to something he doesn't want to do? His explanation involved a consideration for the feelings of the other person. He didn't want to hurt anyone's feelings. Saying yes when he really felt no was just a way to avoid conflict. Of course, we reflected on how this might be a short term solution, but it actually ended up creating more conflict in the long run. Instead of saying "no" at the outset, he spent a great deal of energy making sure his partner felt his desire to say "no" in an indirect way, without having to actually say it.

After talking about it a little more, we discovered another reason for saying yes instead of no, and it had to do with his childhood. If he had said no to his father growing up he would have been shamed and attacked. Saying no to his father would have seemed like an act of rebellion, a declaration of war. It was no wonder that this client found it hard to say no to his partner. This was how he'd been programmed to respond in a relationship.

We began to explore the idea of saying no. We decided if his partner asked him to do something he didn't want to do, he would just say no. Simple, right? It seemed like a good start, but very quickly we ran into a problem. The client's partner reported frustration with the fact that now he was saying no to everything! So we realized we needed to go a little deeper and examine why. We went from the client saying yes to his partner but not really meaning it and then being passive aggressive about it (which caused conflict in their relationship), to the client saying no directly, shutting down the conversation (which also caused conflict), and finally to the client saying no and then explaining why he didn't want to do something. If he was able to explain why he didn't want to go out to dinner at a particular restaurant, or why he didn't want to walk the dog at a particular time in the morning, his partner felt involved and considered, which was exactly what she wanted. In fact, the client remarked how it felt weird to be explaining something the he felt was obvious, when it fact it was completely not obvious to his partner at all.

This was not as easy a process as it sounds here. People who struggle with passive aggressive behavior often find it hard to change because deep down it can be so satisfying. It feels good to nurture a source of anger and resentment. It feels good to fight the noble fight against a person trying to keep us down. It feels good to consider yourself to be the one in the argument who's on the right side of things. But it feels good in the way that an arsonist feels good as he watches a building burn. It's self destructive behavior that has been converted via our childhood experiences into a defense mechanism that is an essential part of us. It can be very hard to learn to say no, and then even more difficult to explain why. But in my experience this path leads to greater intimacy and appreciation between people in relationships. If you feel like this chapter describes you then perhaps it's time to start thinking about say yes less and no more, and most importantly, to talk about why.

FIFTEEN

The (Math) Test

In family therapy we often talk about issues between parents and children, including areas of conflict that have deteriorated to the point where outside help is sought. As in individual or couples therapy, everyday situations that lead to conflict are discussed, and then explored on a deeper emotional level. One of the many high conflict situations that comes up with school age children is the battle over homework. As a parent, I like to share my experience dealing with my kids in situations that reflect what clients are dealing with in their own lives.

Some kids don't like math. Some kids don't like homework. Many kids don't like the combination of math and homework. My daughter is one of these kids. When it came time to do her homework, she would put up a massive fight, screaming and crying and yelling at me. No matter how much I tried to calmly explain to her that the homework needed to be done, that at the very least an effort needed to be made, and that she was capable of doing anything she set her mind to, things didn't change. Our dinner table homework sessions almost always ended with arguing and anger and tears. And my daughter didn't feel so great either.

At first her anger triggered my anger. Here I was, trying to be a good parent, helping her with a difficult subject, being encouraging and patient, and what did I get? Intense, physical, slamming-hands-on-the-table anger. Her anger made me so angry I wanted to overwhelm her anger with my anger. But then I had an insight. I realized that she felt bad about herself because she didn't get math. Her older brother is a math whiz, he made it look easy. For my daughter, it was like pushing a giant boulder up a mountain. I realized that this anger was a defense mechanism for her. When confronted with a subject she couldn't grasp, it made her feel ashamed and like a failure, so she lashed out at me, poking and prodding and pushing me to get so angry with her so that we would have a blow out fight, ending with me sending her to her room, and thus she wouldn't have to do her homework after all. Pretty clever actually.

So I came back with a plan of my own. I redoubled my efforts at patience. I became the Buddha of Beginning Geometry. No matter how mad she got at me, I never lost my cool. Okay, that's a lie. When she stabbed me with a pencil (supposedly an accident) I did get pretty pissed off. But overall, I was pleased with my new reaction to her protests. I imagined myself as a machine built to transform anger into love, yelling into peace, and I tried to take all of her frustration and rage and shame and channel it into myself and then let it flow peacefully away. My main takeaway from this was that instead of trying to change her behavior, I tried to change mine.

Her behavior was predicated on having me to oppose her. Everything she was doing was in opposition to me. I was the one making her do something she didn't want to do, so she fought back against me. My response to this at first was to counter attack her resistance with a show of parental force. To force her feelings to change due to the logic of the situation. To dominate her emotionally and impose my will. My anger could be bigger than her anger.

But the solution ended up being to remove the resistance. At first it was hard not reflect her anger at me back at her, no matter how justified I felt. She would scream and protest in the same old way, but instead of hitting the tennis ball of anger back to her I just let it bounce past me. Over and over again. It was hard at first, but over time it got easier. Without my anger to feed off, her anger withered. Her rage lost steam. Nobody was returning her serve.

As the anger faded, the resistance to homework dwindled. The walls of anger she had built up to protect herself came down, and she started to open up and try. She began to grasp some of the math concepts she had struggled with so much before. Her multiplication tables became something she was proud to show me her progress in. A worksheet that used to take two hours of struggle became a task we could knock out in fifteen minutes. Eventually she would come home from school and take out her math homework and complete it on her own (cue angels singing).

This process took so long I didn't really notice it was happening. It was only at the end that I realized how far we had come. The lesson I learned was that when you find your-self in opposition with someone in a relationship, whether with your child, parent, spouse or partner, sometimes the best way to affect change is to remove the opposition. I don't mean giving up. I don't mean internalizing your resentment while letting the other person win. I mean truly trying to let those feelings of anger and resentment dissipate. By changing your approach you can change the whole situation. You will be surprised how much the people in your life will be willing to change when they see you making your own effort to change first.

SIXTEEN

The Gravity of Addiction

Addiction issues are a common reason people seek therapy. Often times people seek help for issues in their lives that, after some examination, turn out to be related to addiction. In therapy sessions, we explore the conflict and trauma in their lives caused by these addictions. Addiction in this sense can refer to the abuse of drugs, alcohol, sex, exercise, work, or any other activity or substance that can become compulsive and have harmful consequences. One of the many difficult aspects about dealing with addiction is the cycle of withdrawal, where the client is able to abstain for a period of time from these addictive behaviors but eventually falls back into them. This is quite common, and part of the process of change. I like to describe addiction as having its own force of gravity, just like a planet, and in this metaphor we are all pilots of our own individual spaceships passing by these planets on our journeys through life.

Let's imagine that each of the planets in our imaginary

universe represent various sources of addiction. There are planets of alcohol, drugs, exercise, love, sex, work, everything one can become addicted to and engage in compulsively to their own detriment. Many people are able to fly right past these planets without stopping. Some people are able to land and visit, check out the place, and then blast off into space again. However, some of us land on these planets and can't escape. Something about the gravity of these particular planets combined with our own unique emotional history results in us getting stuck on a planet we can't get off of.

Life on this planet might not seem so bad at first. Sometimes we feel like we've discovered a great new planet that we want to stay on forever. We like what we've found here and how it makes us feel. Over time our addictions grow stronger, and the gravity of the planet grows as well, making it much harder to leave than it was when we first arrived. We might try to leave, but feel the pull of the planet's gravity stronger than we thought it would be, and decide it's easier to stay. But we're not happy living on this planet, and deep down wish that we could leave.

With work and support, and a dedication to changing our lives, we are capable of building up the strength necessary to blast off from this planet of addiction. It almost always takes multiple tries and various levels of what we perceive as failure, but this is the process of change. Eventually we can escape this planet's gravity and get back into space, back into the journey of life. We thought this planet was the place to be, that we would never leave, yet here we are, living away from the planet and enjoying it. We're glad to be putting it in our rear view mirror (our spaceships have rear view mirrors).

So we're cruising along through space again, proud of ourselves for not acting on the addictive thoughts that had ruled our lives for so long. Then we see another planet up ahead. It's identical to the planet we just escaped from. It has the same gravitational pull on us, and as we get closer to the planet the pull gets stronger. Part of us knows we don't want to land there, we don't want to revisit the planet, but a bigger part of us remembers what it was like before, the satisfaction of the addiction, the fulfillment of our craving, and we just want to stop by real quick and say hi. As we debate our options the reality is the choice has already been made, as the gravity of addiction is reaching right into the center of our being and grabbing hold, pulling us back down to the surface of the planet.

And so we zoom back down to the planet of addiction and re-engage in the activities we used to do there. We might feel like we can leave whenever we want this time, that since we've experienced the gravity before we can handle it differently this time. And some people can. But most people can't. We stay, engage, regret, and try to blast off again, only to get pulled back to the ground. Sometimes we break free and cruise along through space again, thinking the gravity of addiction is in the past, but then we pass another planet with a similar gravitational pull, and find ourselves drawn to land there, and the process repeats all over again. Other people might have found an adjustment to make on their spaceship that makes them impervious to the gravity of these planets. Some of us are motivated to continue our space journey with pit stops on planets of addiction along the way. Some of us become so consumed that we crash land on these planets and feel stranded there, never to escape.

With more hard work and dedication we can eventually blast back off again. It takes time and effort to build up the force to break free. It's very hard work. We realize now, though, that the hard work doesn't end when we get back into space. The hard work is avoiding these planets in the future. We eventually come to understand that there are some planets we just can't visit, no matter how much we try to create scenarios where we can. Our friends might be able to come and go as they please from these places, but we know we're not capable of that. This is the time to remind ourselves that we enjoy the journey through space more than living on that planet. We're happier this way, and better equipped to fight the power of gravity now that we have experienced it before. We know where that feeling of gravity pulling us towards our addiction will lead, and in that moment we must hold firm and stay the course on our journey.

SEVENTEEN

The Eternal Well of Worry

A nxiety is one of the most common things we discuss in talk therapy. Everyone, to some extent, has anxious thoughts. For some people these thoughts are a slight annoyance; for others they are paralyzing. Some people experience anxiety as a result of fears about external forces like relationships, current events, or work issues. Others experience anxiety as a filter, something about themselves through which they experience everything in their lives in an anxious way. No matter what the roots of our anxiety are, many of us hold these fears deep inside, a source waiting to be drawn from, like a well that never runs dry.

When a client strongly identifies as being anxious and refers to themselves as a worrier, unable to stop thinking about the future and all the bad things that might happen, the image I sometimes describe to them is a well deep inside us, with the water coming from this well representing our anxiety. Each of us has our own well, ready and waiting for us to draw from it.

It's our own personal reserve of anxiety, a place we can come to in order to draw upon the fears, anger, and stress that we have become accustomed to and incorporated into our lives. There's a well worn path that leads to it, a familiar wooden bucket tied to the side of it, and our reflection is always there looking back at us as we stare down into the water.

This well never runs out. We might draw from it to address a particular subject, a hope or fear, but just like no amount of worrying will ever make a problem go away, no amount of water drawn from the well will ever use it all up. Sometimes we binge, drawing bucket after bucket from the well, in the hopes that if we throw ourselves completely into this process we can use it all up. However, even though the water level might go down, and the well might look empty for a moment, eventually the water of worry starts to seep up from the depths, and the well is full once more.

During those peaceful times in our lives when we don't draw from it, the well just sits there peacefully. It doesn't empty or overflow. It maintains a constant level no matter what we do. It maintains a state of fullness inside of us, no matter what's happening in our lives on the outside. This source of worry is always there. But just because the well is there doesn't mean we have to drink from it, right?

That's a very hard thing to just stop doing because we have decided we want to. This process is something we've been doing our entire lives. We are compelled to act the way we are acting, and we're comfortable with the familiarity of the process even if we do not enjoy the result. Like many things out of our control, it is hard to stop ourselves from trying to change something we cannot change, and instead to learn how to accept these things without the struggle of trying to change them. By accepting them we take back the power to feel how we want to feel. Yes, an unexpected bill might trigger our feelings of anxiety regarding money, which have practical modern day implications, as well as sources going back to our childhood that are not specifically about money but more about the emotions behind our relationship to it. This reaction might never change for us. However, if we can accept the well for just being there instead of feeling like we have to drink from it, we might find ourselves feeling differently about it. The well is there whether we drink from it or not. It's not going anywhere. It's not going to overflow. It's not going to recede. It's not going to go away. It's a part of us, a part of our identity. Our lives will go on whether we drink from the eternal well of worry or not. So let's learn to choose not to drink from it. We can acknowledge it without participating in it. There are better ways to stay hydrated!

EIGHTEEN

Relationship Button Pushing

Couples therapy is similar to and yet very different from individual talk therapy. Seeing client as individuals, we focus on their specific issues. Seeing a couple means that the client isn't one person or the other, but the two of them together. The couple is the client. Issues that come up often have their roots in one person's or the other's emotional material, but the work in couples therapy is in examining how that material affects and is reacted to by each member of the couple. Something I hear often in this scenario is one person saying that the other person "really knows how to push my buttons".

Ah, the buttons! The activators of anxiety. The ignitors of anger. Who are we in our relationships if not for our buttons? Often times the things the other person does that push our buttons are normal, everyday, acceptable things. Most often the actions that push buttons are mundane; being late, not making the bed, leaving dishes in the sink, interrupting you in conversation, etc. This makes me think that the control and responsibility over button pushing and its effects lies not with our partners but with ourselves. To try to get your partner to change the way they act to avoid pushing our buttons is a common reaction, but not the most effective one long term. It's up to us to take responsibility for our own button pushing. So how can we do this?

1 - Disconnection: We realize that when our partner doesn't clean the grounds out of the coffee maker, this pushes our buttons. It triggers a rage in us disproportionate to the action that caused it. We take a deep breath, and try to disconnect the wires behind the buttons. We say to ourselves "That's okay, so what, it's just some coffee grounds, I'll clean them out and get on with my life". This usually works in the short term, but the effects don't last. The moment after we disconnect the wires behind our buttons they start growing back, and the anger starts to seep in again, until eventually we're back at square one.

2 - Rewiring: We decide to take more control over the wiring of our buttons. We decide that instead of anger, when this button gets pushed we're going to feel a different emotion. We're going to remind ourselves that sure, we gotta deal with these coffee grounds, but instead of getting angry, why not remind ourselves that if this is the biggest problem in our relationship, we're doing pretty good! We tell ourselves that this is a totally acceptable situation, but this doesn't last either. The reserve of anger from the button pushing is just getting stored up until we can't take it any more and we grab that coffee maker and throw it against the wall where it breaks into a million pieces and the glass shatters and it feels good for a

moment, but then we realize all we did was break our coffee maker.

3 - Muting. This involves burying the wires behind our buttons underneath insulation. This usually involves drugs or alcohol, so that the reaction to seeing the coffee grounds waiting for us to clean them is initially anger, but then quickly replaced by the welcomed knowledge that at least we have that drug or alcohol that will make everything easier to deal with. This can work, but the better it works the worse off our relationship will actually get. Sort of like killing a fly with a machine gun, it solves the problem but the collateral damage only makes things worse.

4 - Button Pusher Removal - The breakup. Removal of the person who we think is responsible for pushing our buttons. We might feel better about this at first, because now our buttons are not being pushed. But the buttons still exist! They might get dusty from misuse, but eventually we are likely to find ourselves in another relationship that eventually gets to a point where our buttons are pushed all over again, so in the long term this is not really a solution at all.

Couples often come into therapy with a list of grievances about their partners. They account for all the ways their partners push their buttons, and how it's making their relationships unbearable. By viewing this situation through the lens of the concept of relationship button pushing, I guide them to focus less on their partners and more on themselves. One couple in particular had an issue that involved parking. When they'd be looking for a parking space on the way to dinner, the driver would get angry when the passenger would point out parking spaces that were available. He felt like she was being controlling, and he resented it. So the driver would reply in a passive aggressive way, feelings would be hurt, and by the time they sat down to dinner this couple was miserable. In an effort to break this pattern, the next time they went out to dinner the passenger tried not pointing out parking spots, holding her tongue even if she spotted the perfect one. However, this only made her even angrier, as she started to resent the idea that she should have to hold her tongue over something that seemed so innocent to her. This resulted in a similar pattern of snarky remarks and passive aggressive behavior, leaving them sitting down to dinner in the same miserable place.

Through a discussion of the situation, and an exploration of the driver's relationship with his own parents, we realized the suggestions about where to park triggered the driver's emotions associated with being in the back seat as his own parents drove. His parents were an argumentative couple, and after a session talking about this we identified how, when the passenger suggested a parking spot, the driver fell right back into the relationship pattern he saw growing up. He saw this exact situation handled with anger, resentment, and passive aggressiveness, and realized he was following this playbook in his own life. We developed a strategy for this, where the next time they drove to dinner the passenger was encouraged to point out a parking spot again, and this time the driver was instructed to take a deep breath and remind himself it's just a parking spot. He worked to let the feelings of anger and resentment he saw in his parents' relationship go, to flow through him and out into the night, leaving him able to park without anger. It took some work, but soon enough they were able to enjoy going out to dinner again. The driver's desires to have the passenger change her behavior transformed into the realization the driver had the power to change his own.

What this demonstrates is that the more we know about our buttons the better prepared we can be when they are pushed. The more aware we are of their existence and reason for being, the more we can learn to change our reactions, and the more we can understand the root cause of the issues the buttons represent. By engaging in this process, over time we will find that our wiring can be modified, and that the buttons we once resented our partner for pushing are within our own power to disconnect.

NINETEEN

The Snow Globe Effect

When I meet with a client for the first time, they are often in a state of crisis. They might be so depressed they can't function in what they consider a normal way, or so anxious they are feeling physical symptoms that scare them, or their relationship has reached a moment of crisis that seems to be a breaking point. The issues they're dealing with might have been worth discussing in therapy for much of the time previous to their crisis, but things weren't bad enough to go to the trouble of finding a therapist, making an appointment, filling out all those forms. Now, however, the shit has hit the fan in a way that makes talking to someone about it worth all the trouble of getting there. In that first session (or sometimes two or three or more) we spend time downloading everything the client is experiencing. It's a "get it off your chest" kind of situation. There are things the client needs to tell someone, and they almost always feel better after telling someone trained to listen to and support them. There's a sense of relief after verbalizing all the thoughts the client has had bouncing around in their head. The thing is, that good feeling usually disappears as soon as they start to think about what they can do to change their situation. Now what do I do? This is where I encourage them to consider not what they can do to change things in the future, but how they can better process what's happening right now.

At this moment there is so much going on in the client's life that it's like a snow globe that has just been shaken up. If we picture our lives as a snow globe's typically bucolic scene of holiday cheer and pastoral landscape, then in our current situation those scenes are now completely obscured by snow. We're stuck in a snowstorm with no idea where we are or how to get to where we want to be. To the client in a state of crisis, the snow is the problem, and they want to get rid of it. But how do you get rid of snow? One person can't make the snow go away. It's an impossible task. But the funny thing about humans is we often get stuck trying to accomplish impossible tasks. A therapist's job is to point this out, and help switch our focus to the tasks that are possible to accomplish.

So what can we do when our lives have become a shaken-up snow globe? I encourage my clients to stop trying to make the snow go away but to instead wait for it to settle. This means accepting the feelings and events that are causing their crisis without the pressure of having to fix them right away. It seems counter intuitive to come to therapy for guidance about one's problems and then be told not to focus on them so much, but it helps. It's part of the process. Think about it as if the mental energy spent on trying to fix things is actually shaking the globe a little more each time. The more we try to get things to settle down the more we kick the snow up and send it swirling around us again. Sometimes the ways in which we try to fix things actually reinforce them.

The source of our unhappiness is not the snow drifting around obscuring our vision, but in the foundation of our bucolic scene that the snowstorm obscures. Something has changed in that scene that has caused this emotional snow-storm. In this situation, we attempt to let go of the burden of trying to fix things and let ourselves be free to just feel things. This is the mental health equivalent of setting the globe down and waiting for the snow to float back down to the ground. Only then can you get a good look at your surroundings and see what exactly caused the snowstorm. In the same way, only once you've accepted the strong emotions and reactions to events that brought you to therapy without feeling you have to fix them can you start to see the sources of these emotions and reactions to them. We wait for the snow to settle, and then it becomes easier to assess the situation, and then we can begin the process of change.

TWENTY

Mindless Fingernail Biting

I bite my fingernails. It's something I've done my entire life. I've been able to quit for periods of time, and at other times it seemed like I always had a finger in my mouth, biting my nails to the point of bleeding. I find myself biting my fingernails more during moments of stress, but it's not like when I'm not stressed out I don't bite them. Fingernail biting is a physical manifestation of anxiety, and even though I'm aware of it and understand it and am even capable of writing a chapter in a book about it, I haven't been able to quit doing it. There are more specific approaches we can use to explore and change activities like fingernail biting, hair pulling, skin picking, or other physical manifestations of anxiety, but in this chapter I want to examine the more general idea of mindlessness.

It doesn't seem like I ever consciously make a decision to start biting my fingernails. It's just something I realize I'm doing in the moment, as if it's an activity I participate in during my normal, resting state. When I realize I'm doing it, I usually stop, put my hands down, look at them, and think about not doing it again. But then, as soon as my mind moves on to other thoughts, I lose track of my hands, and invariably moments later I find myself biting my fingernails again without even thinking about it. And the pattern repeats. Sometimes I'm aware of the pattern and sometimes I'm not. But most of the time it's a combination of the two; I'm aware of the pattern at moments, but as soon as my mind wanders away I become unaware again.

This fingernail biting is the physical manifestation of anxiety. It's what happens when my mind wanders to anxious thoughts. What are these thoughts exactly? In general, I'm worrying about the future, thinking about possible worst case scenarios and how I might handle them. Specifically, I'm thinking about how that bump in the road could have given me a flat tire, and what a drag it would be if I got one, and how I would have to pull over on the side of the highway and yes I do have a spare, but do I have a jack? And would I be able to change the tire by myself? And there would be a good chance I could get hit by a car on the side of the road, some crazy driver not looking where I'm going, so what would be a better way to handle the flat tire? And then I realize I've spent five minutes worrying about something that will probably not happen and the whole time I've been biting my fingernails.

This is mindlessness. Instead of being in the moment, thinking about where I am, who I'm with, and what I'm doing, my mind is busy conjuring up possible disappointing or worrisome events that could happen in the future, leaving my fingers without guidance, free to move up to my mouth where nails are bitten in a robotic fashion. My mind is busy worrying about possible negative future outcomes, while my mouth and fingernails are acting to create very real negative outcomes in the present.

Not everyone who suffers from anxiety bites their fingernails, but everyone who suffers from anxiety focuses on unknown future possibilities to the detriment of the appreciation of their presence in the present. If you find yourself worrying constantly about events out of your control, with a feeling of doom regarding what might happen in the future pervading your everyday life, you're not focusing on the moment at hand. Sometimes if I feel like I'm biting my fingernails too much I'll literally sit on my hands. There's a version of this approach we can do emotionally, sitting on our figurative hands, which serves to keep us focused on the moment at hand, and not picking at our fingers.

TWENTY-ONE

The Mountaintop of the Midlife

Sometimes the topic of conversation in therapy is a factor of the age of the client. One such topic is the idea of middle age, or how it seems to be more popularly called now, the midlife. Many times clients have issues and feelings about reaching this point in their lives which seem unique and specific to their situation. This is certainly the case, but I find clients also get a feeling of relief learning that many people their age are dealing with similar issues.

The midlife is something you don't always see coming. You sort of wake up one day and find yourself there. It happens the way Ernest Hemingway describes going broke: gradually, then suddenly. One day you're in your late 20s, growing into a career, celebrating weddings and births, still in the know about what music is cool, and watching your hair just begin to thin ever so slightly. The next day the music you like is considered old school, your clothes from high school are considered vintage, and the bald spot on the back of your head has grown to meet the receding hairline in the front.

Reaching the mid point of your life is like hiking up a mountain. From birth you grow up at the foot of the mountain, looking up at it looming in the distance, with the knowledge that one day you will set off to climb it. Eventually that day comes, and as you embark on the journey of life you push forward, hiking uphill. Sometimes the path is easy, sometimes it is hard, but no matter how the trail or the view changes, you continue your slow climb.

When you began this climb you were joined by other people your age, friends who were born at the same time and grew up with you, but as you continue the journey you start to separate. At different forks in the road you choose different paths. Every now and then you stop and sit for a spell, taking a rest, admiring the view. Sometimes you hike along a ridge with an amazing view, but you're so busy getting to where you want to go you don't even notice. Sometimes there are rock slides that send you sliding downhill a bit, but then you find a short cut that gets you further up the mountain. Whatever your path, you are always working towards the same goal: to get to the top of the mountain.

As your journey progresses you might find yourself forgetting about the destination. You get so used to climbing that it becomes second nature to you. The burn in your thighs from walking uphill becomes normal. The view of the mountaintop in the distance becomes a familiar sight, something you take for granted. But then one day you get to the top of the mountain, where you admire the view, catch your breath, and then think: Now what?

For most of us, what happens next is a serious assessment of our lives at this point. After all this focus on the climb we now have a moment to get introspective and look within, taking stock of where we are, how we got here, and how we feel about it. We've reached the mountaintop, but is it the right mountaintop? Is it the mountaintop we pictured this whole time? The fact is the place you've reached at the top of this mountain is most likely not where you pictured yourself ending up when you started your journey. This difference between where you thought you were going and where you actually ended up can be the source of much of the anxiety we associate with the idea of a mid-life crisis.

Imagine you've reached the top of the mountain of the midlife and you're standing there taking stock of where you stand. You might find yourself on a boulder in a rocky outcropping, or in a grassy meadow atop a plateau, or on a dry, dusty ledge. You might find yourself alone, or with a hiking partner. You might be happy with where you are, or you might not be satisfied with where you find yourself. So you look back at the direction you came from, second guessing the choices you made to get here, wishing you had taken a different route. You get so preoccupied with analyzing the choices you made along the way that you neglect to consider the path in front of you. You've spent so much time working towards the goal of reaching the mountaintop you can't imagine dedicating that kind of energy to the path down the other side. In fact, you're not even thinking about the way down. You're still fixated on the way up, even though that part of your journey has come to an end.

There's a clock ticking this whole time, by the way. You

can't just remain on this spot on the mountaintop considering all this. It's like there's a giant invisible hand behind you, gently pushing you downhill. It's ironic because you could have used the support of this invisible hand while you were climbing uphill, and you don't really need it going down. If you haven't been able to accept where you've found yourself on the mountaintop, then you're not going to be aware of the invisible hand pushing you down the other side of the mountain. Your heels will be dug in, dragging in the dirt. Your focus will be on the path behind you instead of the one in front of you, and this will make for an unpleasant journey. If you're not careful you'll find yourself fully feeling the stress and unhappiness behind this conflict for the rest of your life without even realizing what's causing it. And that would be a shame, because the journey down the other side of the mountain has the possibility to be wonderful. The views on the way down are just as scenic as the ones on the way up!

When you've accepted the contradiction between where you thought you'd be and where you are, it can be much easier to enjoy the second half of the journey of your life. You know where you're going now, after all. Unlike your hike up to the top of the mountain, there's only one destination for all of us at this point. We're all eventually going to get to the flat ground on the other side of the mountain. So why not enjoy the rest of the journey? Accept where you're starting from and walk downhill with a spring in your step. Instead of kicking yourself for the choices you made on the way up, take pleasure in making new choices on the way down. Keep your gaze steady on the path ahead of you, not the one behind you.

TWENTY-TWO

Dude, Where Are My Keys?

P eople often ask me what exactly it is I do. It doesn't always satisfy their question when I say that I talk to people about their problems, or provide a safe place for them to vent, or process past emotional trauma. To better explain the work I do, I sometimes tell them a story. It's based on a parable attributed to the Sufi mystic Nasrudin. It's also attributed to Noam Chomsky. It can also be found in various forms in numerous American newspapers going back all the way to the 1920s. It goes like this:

A policeman was walking his beat one night when he came upon a drunk man searching around on the ground underneath a streetlight. The policeman asked the drunk man what he was doing. The drunk man said he was looking for his keys. The policeman started to help him look for the keys, but they couldn't find them. The streetlight shined brightly on the ground, but there were clearly no keys anywhere to be seen. After a few minutes the policeman asked the drunk man if was sure he had lost his keys around there. The drunk man said no, he actually dropped them a couple of blocks back, but the light was better here.

I love this story! It's so simple and clear. To me, it speaks to how we can find ourselves searching for meaning, for answers, for help, but doing it in our own little patch of brightly lit pavement without realizing the keys we are looking for lie elsewhere. It's bright and safe here, it's a comfortable place to look. To go off and look in the darkness and the unknown would be scary. Much safer to stay in the light!

Another reason why we tend to look where we know the thing we're searching for is not is that looking for something gives us a purpose, and it can feel satisfying to engage in this process. This act of searching feels good in and of itself. This process of searching can even be more satisfying than the end goal of finding. I think this is because searching is open ended and full of possibility, while finding means we have to deal with what we have found. And this is where a therapist can be a great help. The therapist is your guide to this search. Let's continue the parable with this in mind.

As the drunk man continued to search for his keys, the policeman got a call about a robbery in progress and left. Then a stranger showed up, carrying a flashlight. The drunk man explained his situation, and the stranger offered to help by walking back up the block with him to help search for the keys where they were actually dropped. The drunk man was apprehensive about this. The events that led to him losing his keys were blurry. He had some vague memories of getting into a fight, of yelling and screaming, of experiencing emotions he would rather not feel again, and which he had intended to suppress by getting drunk in the first place. The stranger gently encouraged him to be brave, and he promised he would be there with him every step of the way to support him. Even though it generated feelings of fear, it made sense to look for the keys where they were actually lost, didn't it? The drunk man had to admit it did.

So the drunk man and the stranger walked back up the street, side by side, the stranger shining his flashlight at the road ahead of them. The drunk man was nervous, but with the stranger's help he retraced his steps, navigating the route back towards where he dropped his keys. Eventually they reached a dark, isolated street corner leading to a dead end. The drunk man felt a wave of anxiety surge through him, a sick feeling in the pit of his stomach, and he turned to leave but the stranger stood behind him, urging him to go on, and then handed him the flashlight.

The drunk man took a deep breath and shined the flashlight around the dead end. It was cold and uninviting, there was graffiti on the walls, and trash littered the street. Then the flashlight revealed a dog, a dirty mutt, crouched in corner, growling. The drunk man's first instinct was to drop the flashlight and run, but the next feeling he had after this urge was the safety of having the stranger with him. He turned to see the stranger still standing next to him, a supportive look on his face, a gentle nod to continue on, so the drunk man turned and faced the dog. The dog growled threateningly, but didn't make a move towards him. The drunk man stood there studying the dog, and eventually realized it seemed familiar to him. He remembered this dog from the past, and in that past the dog wasn't angry and threatening. It was a gentle pet, a friend. He used to pet the dog and it would lick his hand play-fully, but then because of some traumatic event in the past things changed and the dog became angry and dangerous. As the drunk man experienced this memory the dog stopped barking and started to wag its tail. Emboldened, the drunk man approached the dog, holding out his hand. The dog tentatively came towards him and sniffed the drunk man's hand, then yelped playfully and rubbed up against him. The drunk man felt a wave of relief wash over him as he petted the dog, remembering all the good times they had spent together before things changed.

The stranger placed a gentle hand on the drunk man's shoulder and pointed over to where the dog had been sitting. The drunk man looked over and saw, up against the curb, the lost keys. He picked them up, looking at them as if seeing them for the first time, feeing a sense of accomplishment he hadn't felt in ages. He turned to the stranger to thank him for his help, but the stranger demurred, telling him all he did was walk beside him. It was the drunk man who was brave enough to undertake the journey.

We each have our own metaphorical keys, and we've all lost those keys at some point in our lives. Sometimes we lose them in places we don't want to go, so we look for them where we feel safe. We might feel good in the act of looking for them under the brightness of a streetlight, but we won't find them there. It's hard to confront our past, especially when we've spent a good chunk of our lives trying to forget it. We all have growling dogs lurking in the darkness of a time we don't want to remember, but if not examined and confronted, the fear of these dogs will determine how we live our lives in the present, often with a negative influence.

It makes sense that part of us doesn't want to find the keys, because it can be scary. Logic doesn't apply in this situation. It makes sense to think that we would look for our keys where we dropped them, but our mind is excellent at using emotion to twist logic and protect ourselves from pain. The pain lies in the darkness and it hides the truth, but it's the truth we need to find because through confronting it we will be able to finally open the door that can lead us to a happier place.

TWENTY-THREE

The Hamster of Love

My daughter has a pet hamster. Which means I have a pet hamster. She is a cute little dwarf hamster, a great pet, relatively easy to care for, not too much poop and pee, and did I mention she's really cute? She eats nuts, which is great, because I hear nuts are good for you, so whenever I put some almond slivers in her cage I have some too. She is docile and easy to handle, and doesn't run away when you pick her up. Her cage is across the room from my desk, and I can hear and see her while I'm working. She's super cute. We used to have a great relationship.

I say used to because eventually things changed. I used to enjoy taking her out of her cage and holding her, petting her, or putting her on my desk while I was working. But then one time I went to take her out of her cage and she bit me. Not a strong bite, not nearly hard enough to draw blood, but enough of a nip to make me yank my hand away. It surprised me more than it hurt. And even though it didn't really hurt that much, it was enough to make me rethink taking her out and cuddling with her. I just closed the cage, talked to her a little, and then went back to work. It didn't seem like a big deal at the time but things had changed between us.

The next day as I sat at my desk I looked over at the cute little hamster who was sitting in her cage looking back at me. I thought about taking her out and playing with her, but then I remembered the bite she gave me and had second thoughts. You see, I have an aversion to animals biting me. In fact, it took me a couple of days to build up the desire to try again. But this time I was prepared. I decided I wasn't going to flinch. I would let her take a little nip at my thumb, try not to react, and let her warm up to me. Maybe this was part of her process, a quick moment of self defense, and then a removal of defenses so we could cuddle again. I was going to be the bigger mammal. So, I put my hand in her cage, let her sniff my fingers, and after a moment of pawing and sniffing, she nipped me. I didn't flinch, though. I was pretty proud of myself, too. I was happy with the process, and about to pick her up, when she bit me. And this time it was definitely a bite. It hurt. It drew a little blood. And this time I yelped in pain and yanked my hand away. I might have even yelled something like "Bad hamster!". I went and sprayed some Bactine on it, put on a bandage, and went back to my desk. I was still pretty mad, and looked over to see this cute little hamster looking back at me, innocent and pure, like she didn't do anything wrong. But had she done something wrong? Or had she just done something hamster-ish? Either way, there was a rupture in our relationship. Things had changed between me and my hamster.

I wasn't quite ready to give up on her, though, so I did a little research and found that dwarf hamsters, after not having been handled in a while, will sometimes start to bite like this. Apparently it's a common occurrence. The more time that elapses between loving moments of being picked up and held the more likely they are to bite. It can take some time for them to get used to being handled again after some time not being handled. The hamster owner just has to be patient and let the hamster warm up again. That made sense. However, I was still hurt, and didn't want to give her a chance to warm up again. Did she really deserve it? Here I am, just trying to love her, and she hurts me. I resented her.

This made me realize my relationship with my hamster mimicked what many of our romantic relationships are like. Many of us bite our partners when they reach out to us, driving them away and leaving us alone, looking cute while we stuff our cheeks with almond slivers. I know my hamster wants to be picked up and cuddled, to be loved, but her instinct is to protect herself by biting. Many people in relationships have some deep feelings of fear or shame or some other strong emotions that they have a hard time being vulnerable with. What does this mean, to be vulnerable? It means to share your deepest emotions and fears. To reveal your true self to your partner in a way that brings you closer together. On a conscious level we want love, we want our partner to reach into our cage and take us out and cuddle with us. On a subconscious level, we might feel like we don't deserve this love, that we're not worth it, and this feeling is expressed as anger in response to the love we are shown, and therefore we bite. We bite to establish some distance between us and our partners, so we don't have to confront the shame or fear or other strong emotions that bubbles up when we get really close to someone and start to reveal our true selves in a vulnerable way.

How did I react to my hamster biting me? I got angry and removed myself from interacting with her. But did the hamster really want this? I don't think she did. She continues to look at me from her cage with what I now consider a look of longing, but I'm afraid if I engage with her she'll bite me. So now I don't cuddle with her. I feed her, change her cage, and do all the things I usually do to continue our relationship, but we're not as close as we could be. So, our relationship has reached a stopping point. We can't grow any closer now. She's protecting herself, and I've learned not to reach out to her in the ways I had in the past.

Does this dynamic seem familiar? I think it's more common than people realize. It's so, so hard to be vulnerable with the deep rooted emotions that we have learned to protect at all costs over the course of our lives. Then along come romantic partners who want nothing more than to love us for who we truly are. And that's what we want, right? I would say yes. The hamster related irony here is that another part of us says no, and bites. If you can relate to this process, think about how you bite and why you bite. Or how your partner bites and why they bite. Relationships sometimes involve more biting than cuddling, whether we're talking about humans or hamsters!

.   .   .

UPDATE Mel (the hamster) and I have made up, and she is letting me hold her again without biting me!

TWENTY-FOUR

The Career Ladder

Clients in their 20s often want help processing issues regarding their careers. That decade of our lives is usually where we're right in the middle of having our decisions regarding what we do for work really start to define who we are and how we identify ourselves. For many of us, our career defines us. It's the answer to the common question, "What do you do?". This question can easily be the spark that kicks off a brush fire of anxiety inside us. We do something, don't we? Of course we do. But what if what we do is something we don't really love doing? We might not want to be defined by what we currently do. So do we answer with what we currently do, or what we hope to do someday? Do we even know what we hope to do someday? We might do many things that bring us different levels of satisfaction, but then how to explain that? In the not so recent past, people went to school to study to work in certain fields, and then got jobs in those fields, and then worked at those jobs until they retired. Nowadays things aren't so simple. The chances of working for the same company your whole career, or even staying in the same career, are much smaller than ever before. The question of "What do you do?" has changed in its meaning and significance to our definition of ourselves.

I think that, while this question itself is not going to change, over time the answers will. Or more specifically, society's expectations for the answers to this question will change. Nowadays people are more likely to have multiple careers throughout their lives, often at the same time. As you start out on the path of your working life you're likely to try out different jobs at different stages of different careers. I think an important part of this process is giving yourself permission to answer the "What do you do" question honestly and without judgement of yourself. You shouldn't feel like you have to pick a career and then spend your working life staying in your lane. And that's where the ladder metaphor comes in.

I was speaking to a young man just starting out in the entertainment field. He knew he wanted to work in the business, but he wasn't sure how exactly. He liked writing and being creative on his own, but he also enjoyed the business side of things, working in a group environment. He was interested in being a writer, and a producer, and an executive, and an agent. The concern he shared with me was about choosing a career ladder to start to climb. How could he be sure that one of these ladders was really the one he wanted? He felt like he needed to know which ladder was right for him before he invested the time and energy necessary to start to advance up the rungs of his chosen career.

The career ladder. A classic metaphor. What makes sense

about it to me is the idea that there are rungs on a ladder, just like there are levels of responsibility in a career. For this young man, the career rungs were positions of responsibility: intern, assistant, manager, junior executive, associate vice president, senior vice president, president. What doesn't make sense to me is that the ladder is an isolated concept that only represents one career path, as well as the fact that the higher up on the ladder you get, the harder it is to get off, much less switch ladders.

I could tell that this young man felt the same way without quite being able to verbalize it. We talked about how how this ladder metaphor was flawed. For starters, the idea of choosing from different career ladders implied that the choice of one eliminated the options of any of the others. Another flaw was the concept of climbing up the rungs, getting higher and higher up on the ladder, to the point where it was dangerous. This implies that if you fall from the ladder, you end up down at the bottom of the ladder and have to start all over. In addition, once you're up there high enough on the ladder you can't reach out and try climbing a different ladder. The higher up you go on the ladder, the harder it is to switch ladders. And the idea of climbing two ladders at once is in complete violation of basic ladder safety (see www.americanladderinstitute.org/page/BasicLadderSafety).

As we discussed the ladder metaphor and this young man's hopes and fears regarding it, I started to think about a different metaphor for the professional career he was about to embark on. I feel like the concept of the career path makes more sense, but with the idea that these paths shouldn't be thought of as individual, isolated choices. I see his career path starting out in the same place as many of his contemporaries, but not as an isolated, independent route towards the end goal fo his chosen career. I encouraged him to avoid the tunnel vision that I had experienced in my professional life. I broke in to the entertainment business as a comedy writer, and I was lucky to have enough success that it sustained me financially. My regret is that I had career blinders on that prevented me from seeing any other opportunities. I was so happy to have had success as a comedy writer, to have an identity that was a simple answer to the "What do you do?" question, that I lost all curiosity regarding any other career paths. And thus, later on in my career when work had slowed down and I began to realize I wasn't going to spend my whole life writing tv comedy, I found I didn't have any other interests or opportunities I could immediately switch my focus towards. I was high up enough on my career ladder that it was scary to think about jumping over to another one. After years of climbing it was a long way down if I fell! So at this point in my life I started testing the waters, reaching out to friends and contemporaries who worked in similar but different fields, and as I did this I realized I wished I have been doing this my whole career.

And that's what I encouraged this young man to do. Instead of thinking about himself climbing rungs on a ladder, think about it as walking a path. And from this path he will be able to see other paths similar to his, as well as the ability to examine these other paths as they pass near each other. Instead of being on a career ladder where, if he wants to switch to another career ladder he risks falling to the ground and having to start all over, he should think about it more like he has the ability to step onto another path as they cross and overlap. How does this manifest in the real world? By being curious. During his work experience he's going to run into people with similar but different career paths, and he should be curious about what their experiences are like, about where their paths started and how they have led them to this moment in time. Instead of having blinders on, focussing only on the path ahead of him, he should also be looking around him. Get out of the career path comfort zone and be curious about what other people do, because you might just find yourself interested in something you never thought you'd be interested in, but turns out to be the perfect career for you.

TWENTY-FIVE

We Build Our Own Cages

One of the aspects of talk therapy clients I work with appreciate learning about is the idea that they have the power to determine their own happiness. They often come into therapy blaming external forces for making them feel the way they feel, but through the course of our work together they start to appreciate how they have been outsourcing the control of their emotions to other people. Then they learn how to take the power back.

Once upon a time there was a man who felt alone. He craved relationships, friendship, social interaction. He wanted his life to be like a beer commercial, full of meeting friends after work, music festivals on the weekends, parties and smiles and high fives by the pool. Only his life wasn't anything like this. After a long day at work all he really wanted to do was go home and watch tv on his couch. On the weekends he liked to sleep in and go for long hikes by himself. Sometimes on a Saturday night if he didn't have plans he would scroll through his phone, looking for people to connect with, but this made him feel needy and desperate in the eyes of others. Part of him wanted to be the guy with lots of friends and social gatherings, but another part of himself wanted to stay at home by himself. This conflict resulted in quite of bit of anxiety. He often felt unhappy with his life.

Once upon another time there was a woman who had a great career. She was smart and driven and worked hard to get to a place where she had a job that was well paying, with a great deal of responsibility, and doing this job was fulfilling to her. However, she constantly felt like she was missing out on getting married and starting a family. She went on Bumble dates, was set up by friends, and had several relationships that had potential to develop into the life she wanted, but she always ended up finding a reason why they were doomed to failure. She prioritized work and career over romance and relationships, and even though she enjoyed going to work every day, at the same time she cursed her job since it seemed to be in direct conflict to her ability to dedicate time to a relationship and to starting a family. It was in her power to cut back on work and focus on other things, but she truly enjoyed her work and made it a priority over everything else in her life. She felt strongly conflicted about these two opposing drives.

Maybe you know someone like these two people. Maybe you yourself are like them. You might recognize parts of yourself in their stories. This is a common phenomenon many of us experience in our lives. It's the clash between what we think we should want and what we actually want, and it can be a great source of unhappiness. If left alone, without examination or awareness, we can go our whole lives with this deep rooted feeling of unhappiness, no matter what happens to us or what plans we make. It's as if each of us constructs a cage specific to our own fears and desires. They're the same for all of us in that they prevent us from getting outside of this cage to engage in the experiences that lie beyond our reach that could bring us happiness. They're also unique in that these cages are built of material taken from our own specific emotional history. Our cages have the same general dimensions, but are built to our own personal specifications.

These cages are something we examine in therapy. Many times we can observe a defense mechanism at work. Our feelings of low self esteem make us afraid to put ourselves out there to our friends, to reach out and reveal we are lonely, so instead we don't reach out and instead pine for the outcome of reaching out but can't get past the risk of rejection, and end up alone. We crave a partner and a life defined by family relationships instead of work success, but we fear the commitment, the responsibility, the chances of failure. Maybe our own childhood family experience wasn't supportive or nurturing enough, so instead of trying to create our own adult family experience we don't try for fear of failing. Whatever reason we have for making these delicate, personalized cages, they are a source of unhappiness, and worth examination.

How can we escape this cage? Like most things in this book, the first step is being aware of the cage. Many of us in this situation don't realize we are in cages at all. We reach out through the bars, craving what is beyond our reach without realizing we have the power to escape on our own, that we have the key to unlock the door. The question this brings up is: What do we really want? Do we really want a life full of social interaction and plans with friends? Or do we just feel like we should want that? Do we really want to settle down and start a family? Or do we just feel like we should want this? Maybe we really want these things but are afraid of them, and thus constructed this cage to keep us from having to deal with this. Maybe it's okay if we enjoy spending time alone and don't have a large circle of friends. Maybe it's okay if we love our work and prefer to dedicate our time and energy to that instead of starting a family.

Once we realize we're living in a cage of our own construction, we need to examine it and discuss it, either in therapy or with our friends or loved ones. What about the possibilities on the outside of the cage scares us? What exists inside the cage that makes us feel comfortable? Perhaps this introspection will result in us embracing our fears and striking out into the world beyond the cage, where we'll discover happiness beyond the fear. Or maybe we'll realize what we think we want isn't what we really want at all, and our cage will cease to be a place of detention and evolve into a nest where we can live in happiness and satisfaction. Either option sounds pretty good, right? That's because we're breaking a pattern. We're seeing how our lives have slowly evolved into a situation that has become a source of anxiety and unhappiness. We're thinking about and talking about and considering our conflicting drives and desires, and how we can embrace or shed them in order to live happier lives. No matter how elaborate the cage, ultimately we have the key within ourselves.

TWENTY-SIX

Story of My Life

Sometimes clients have to change therapists. They might be receiving free or reduced price mental health care at a university or training site, and when the student or trainee therapist they work with graduates or moves on to private practice, they are assigned a new therapist. I was in this situation once with a client who was disappointed with having to make this change. As he put it, he didn't look forward to having to recount "The Story of His Life" to his new therapist. He didn't want to have to catch them up about who he is, what brought him to therapy, the work he and I had done together, etc. He wanted to be able to just yadda yadda yadda his way past all that. We spent a good portion of our last session talking about the reaction he was having. Why was he feeling this resistance to telling his story to a new person? Why was he so sick of telling it? We both agreed that these feelings of negativity were not the ideal way to start off with his new therapist, so we decided to try to find something positive about the transition.

I encouraged this client to look at the first session with his new therapist not as an annoying task in having to retell his story, but as an exciting opportunity to pitch himself as he wanted to be seen. This was a chance to experience how he could shape the narrative of his own story. He had been telling himself pretty much the same Story of His Life for as long as he could remember, but based on the work we had done together up until that point he had changed, and so we needed to examine how his story had changed, and if we were being true to it as we imagined retelling it.

This client was a fan of Marvel comics and movies, so we thought about his situation as if she were the main character in a comic series written decades ago, and how many things about it we would change to bring it up to date. We might see that the setting of the story needs to change. Our hero's goals and desires might have changed. The put upon sad sack lead character might end up becoming more of an admirable heroic type. The villain who was a barrier to future happiness might have turned out to be an ally. The situation might have gone from No End In Sight to Light At the End of the Tunnel. In this new version of the story, there were more reasons for our hero to be happy than sad. And the idea here is that it's hard to appreciate if any of these things about you have changed if you're just flipping through the pages, skimming the story of your life mindlessly, repeating how it's always been, instead of really considering how your life has changed and how you now reflect all this personal growth you've been experienced. Sometimes our stories change but we don't notice as we continue on with the same words we've always told ourselves.

The transition between therapists is a great way for a client to reassess their own emotional journey in this way, but once you're aware of this concept anytime is a good time to review your story. This is especially true when you meet new people. Often times the people closest to us, the ones we spend the most time with, they have been familiar with our story since the beginning, and can't see us as anything beyond the character we were introduced to them as. This in turn is reflected in our attitudes about ourselves. If other people expect us to continue with the same story, why shouldn't we expect ourselves to have a different one?

The client ended up excited by the end of hour session. Instead of feeling like it was a drag to catch the new therapist up on his situation, he saw it as a chance to share how much he'd learned about himself, and say out loud to a new person what he'd been through and what he'd overcome. It made him proud, like he had changed for the better, and it turned out to be a great way to end our clinical relationship.

So think about your story. Be conscious of how you present yourself. Listen to how you describe yourself, both in conversation with others and in your own mind. Be curious about noticing the things about you that have changed. When you're around the same people all the time, you might not feel like anything about you is changing. Sometimes in telling your story to someone new you will discover things about yourself that have changed for the better, and you'll be proud of them, and this experience will reinforce your desire to continue working on yourself to make more positive changes.

TWENTY-SEVEN

I (Don't) Like Big Buts

Clients I see in talk therapy often describe things they said to their romantic partners that either caused or exacerbated moments of relationship conflict (otherwise known as fights), and then explain the reasoning behind their actions. It usually sounds something like, I did X and said Y, which hurt their feelings, BUT here is why I'm actually justified in what I said and did. What comes before the BUT is what we admit is true, but what comes after the BUT negates it. And what comes after the BUT is almost always the justification for an action or statement that their partner did not respond well to, and that very likely our client knew their partner would not respond well to. We use these BUTS to justify behavior we feel like we need to justify, which usually means it's behavior that deep down inside we know we'd be better off not engaging in. There are BUTS in all aspects of our lives, but it's the relationship BUTS that are the biggest BUTS.

One way our BUTS get in the way in our relationships is when we say something like, I know you don't like it when I do X, BUT this is why I am justified in doing it. Or, I know I said I wouldn't do X anymore, BUT let me explain why it's actually okay that I did. You asked me not to do something, BUT here's why I have to do that thing, and the reasons why you shouldn't be angry. This is where we acknowledge that we know we're doing something our partner doesn't like us doing, but we continue to do it anyways. We think we can reason our way out of responsibility for doing something that hurts our partner, but we can't. In our minds we might be shifting responsibility for our actions to our partner, but to our partner we are not. We might feel we are in the right, and that being in the right is enough reason to do anything, but even when we are right we can make our relationships feel wrong.

Another way our BUTS get in the way is when we say I'm sorry, BUT. I'm not talking about the I'm sorry BUT I asked for no pickles. I mean more like I'm sorry BUT I had to do it. I'm sorry BUT here's why you're wrong. I'm sorry BUT everyone else was doing it. We're using an apology to justify saying something we feel we need justification for. We're using reason to deal with an emotional situation, and no amount of logical justification will change our emotions.

Then there's the big one: I love you, BUT. This one is a killer. Here the BUT completely negates what comes before it. From your point of view, it might seem like constructive criticism for your partner given in a gentle, caring way. I love you, BUT could you change this one thing? Being on the receiving end of this hurts. You're saying you love them, but the BUT means you don't really love them that much, because someone who really loved them would accept their faults instead of pointing them out.

There's also the classic "make up a good thing so you can say a bad thing" move. I like X, BUT I really don't like Y. Or, it's nice that you did X, BUT I really would have preferred Z. Do you really like X? No, you don't like X. BUT you have something to say about what you don't like, and you want to soften the perceived blow.

The thing I work on with my clients in this situation is to stop talking before the BUT. Just stop after the first half of the sentence. CUT THE BUT. And that means no fancy alternatives to BUT. You can't bust out the thesaurus and replace BUT with HOWEVER, STILL, YET, NEVERTHELESS, or NOTWITHSTANDING. It's common for this to turn into a game of verbal limbo, twisting what we want to say into a different form to make it acceptable. That's why I prefer the idea of stopping before the BUT. This will make you reconsider both what you really want to say, and what you say before you say what you really want to say.

So when you next find yourself in this situation and you stop before the BUT, we'll see if you can be sorry without negating it. Allow yourself to feel exposed without undercutting it. Now you can really consider how what you want to say will affect your partner, and in considering that you might zero in more on what you want to say and be able to express it better. See how your partner reacts to the elimination of what follows the BUT. Learn to not like big BUTS!

TWENTY-EIGHT

Relationship Autopilot

One of the things people come to talk therapy for help with is repeating negative patterns in their relationships. Often a client will describe a fight with their partner that is emblematic of the issues they want to change about themselves. They'll describe the fight, and after a few sessions and some self reflection, they will start to develop a better understanding of what they're doing and why they're doing it. However, that doesn't mean they are suddenly able to change. The patterns they're describing have been going on their entire lives, and that's something to consider when we talk about trying to change them. It's like trying to turn an ocean liner; it starts small, takes time, and happens gradually. The first stage of this change is an awareness of the patterns we want to change, but initially this awareness is frustrating because we can't act on it. We might feel like we know what we want to change but some part of ourselves refuses to listen and we're powerless to stop it. It's like we're on relationship autopilot.

It might play out something like this: You have a fight with your partner, and you fall into your pattern. You react a certain way, they react a certain way, the typical dynamic kicks in, the same feelings emerge, and the night is ruined. And as this is happening, part of you is recognizing exactly what's happening and wants to avoid it. This part of you is like a captain trying to steer a cruise ship away from an iceberg but unable to change course. This part of you is helpless, and watches as the fight plays out in the predictable pattern, resulting in the predicable relationship conflict and resulting unhappiness. This phase of development can be super frustrating. It's like you're watching yourself do something you know you don't want to do but you still do it. Like a horror movie, where you're yelling at the actor to not go into that creepy old house, that it will only end badly, but they still go into that creepy old house and it of course ends badly. Only later on, after the blow up, is the captain able to regain control of the ship, and only then are you capable of approaching your partner and apologizing. You might even explain that you knew what you were doing and that you didn't want to be doing it but that you felt powerless to stop doing it.

As you work through this process, both the actual fights and the therapy sessions talking about the fights, the captain will start to get more control of the ship. Soon you might be able to actually stop at some point during the next fight as the pattern is playing out and state that you don't want to act like this, that you don't want this pattern to continue (even as the pattern continues). In a peaceful moment at a different time, you might be able to explain to your partner what you are doing in your fights and why you're doing it, acknowledging that you know it's making you both unhappy and that you just don't know how to stop it. An awareness of the destructive patterns that make our relationships unhappy is a huge step along the road to change, but it's a frustrating one because we can finally see that the person responsible for our unhappiness is ourselves. We should be the one person who we have the most control over, yet we often find it so hard to make ourselves change.

Eventually the captain starts to regain control earlier and earlier in the pattern. Where at first they could only right the ship after the fight was already over, they begin to be able to do this earlier in the process. The fights get shorter and shorter as the resolution moves up little by little. The end goal is to find yourself in the same situation, with same issues and the same conflict and the same patterns about to be followed, but this time we are able to choose to act differently. The trigger that kicks in our defensive emotions and starts the process we are trying to change suddenly doesn't work. We find ourselves in full control of the ship, realizing that usually we would react a certain way, but we finally feel like we have the option not to. Instead, we might verbalize exactly what's happening, acknowledging that we would usually react a certain way but this time we are not. And we might also get positive feedback from our partner, an appreciation for the change we have worked so hard to achieve. The relationship autopilot is finally disabled, but for all the trouble it caused there was one thing about autopilot that was good: We didn't have to do anything! Now we find ourselves in a much more active role, having to work hard at doing the things we need to do to have less conflict and more connection in our relationship. The cruise control is off, meaning we have to keep our eyes on the road and our hands on the wheel, and even though this takes more effort, it leads to a closer and more satisfying relationship.

TWENTY-NINE

Emotional Deep Tissue Massage

Clients I work with in talk therapy don't always want to engage with the issues that have brought them to therapy. Sometimes these issues are so painful that they spend a great deal of mental and emotional energy avoiding them, convincing themselves they are here to talk about something else, something less painful, although this less painful issue is usually indirectly caused by the more painful issue. In this sense, working with a therapist is like getting a deep tissue massage. Sometimes the most painful parts of ourselves are the parts that need attention the most.

I used to go to this Korean spa in my old neighborhood where the masseuses had an uncanny knack for finding that area of my back that was the most painful to work on. I would squirm on the table, trying to move in a way that would protect the sore spots, but it was no use. The masseuse always found these spots and worked on them, and although it hurt in the moment, afterwards my back felt better. Talk therapy is like getting a deep tissue massage. We come to therapy with a sore spot, something causing us pain, and the therapist helps us identify and work on it. We might want to avoid talking about this subject in order to avoid the pain of addressing it, but with the therapist's guidance we do this, and although it hurts in the moment, we feel better afterwards, often with a new understanding of ourselves. For a little while, at least. Until the next accumulation of physical and emotional stress eventually send us back in search of treatment.

Often times a client will come into therapy with an idea of what is causing their pain, in the same way that you might go in for a massage and tell the masseuse you want them to focus on your shoulders because that's where you carry all your tension. Once they get in and start working, however, the source of pain is revealed to be something different than what we thought it was. The masseuse starts out on our shoulders but moves down into our back and finds a sore spot there that's the real source of all the tension. In the same way, a therapist works with the client to consider different aspects of their lives than the ones they came in prioritizing, and helps to recognize what's really causing them the pain that's brought them to seek treatment.

The avoidance of painful subjects is an example of a concept called *resistance*. In this scenario, resistance is exhibited by actions such as subtly changing the subject whenever a particular area is mentioned, or even point blank declaring that a particular subject is considered off limits. It's the feelings that happen when someone brings up a sensitive subject, both the emotional reactions and the physical. We might stiffen up, sit up a little straighter, clear our throats. We might say things like "Anyways…" or "But back to your question…" or "yadda yadda yadda". This is the therapeutic equivalent of squirming on the massage table. Avoiding the hands of the masseuse digging into that one painful spot on our back. The irony is, the spot we want to avoid dealing with is the one that we stand to gain the most from dealing with.

What causes this sore spot in the first place? In our back, muscles might lock up to protect an area injured in a fall, which can set off a chain reaction of other muscles reacting until one gets strained too far. That's when we end up hobbling in to see our masseuse, desperate for immediate relief. In our lives, we will experience trauma that leads us to develop defense mechanisms to deal with trauma, to protect ourselves from feeling these strong feelings. These defense mechanisms can set off a chain reactions of other emotional reactions until one gets strained too far and starts to affect our lives in a way that we recognize we're not happy with and want to change.

Don't let this idea of embracing the parts of you that scare you the most scare you too much. Most therapists are not going to force you to talk about something you don't want to talk about. No masseuse would ever physically hold you down and force you to accept their elbow in the most sensitive part of your back if you said you didn't want that. But in both cases, the sore spot is mentioned and considered, not ignored. And if we're not ready to address it this time, maybe next time. Or the time after that. But eventually, to change our lives in the most positive way, we need to address the most painful spots in our backs and ourselves.

THIRTY

The Safety of the Path

M aking big changes in our lives can be a scary thing to consider. It is so much easier not to change. The possibility of being happy in a different situation is often outweighed by the relief of staying put and not having to deal. It's situations like this that can lead to us feeling stuck. And it's not just dealing with change we're talking about here. It's also the kinds of lives people lead as they avoid change. How much unhappiness are we willing to accept in our lives in order to avoid having to make big changes.

What does it mean to feel stuck? It usually means we're unhappy with the way things are, but we don't see anything changing anytime soon. It's like we're hiking on a path in a forest. The path is worn and clear, and all around us the forest is thick and overgrown, so the easiest way forward is this path we're already on. But this path sort of sucks. It's got lots of roots to stumble over, it seems to be always going uphill, there's

muddy spots we get stuck in, and we can never see quite far
enough ahead to know where we're going. Even though we
don't like this path, there seems to be no other alternative. It's
our only option.

At least it appears to be our only option. It's not impossible
to get off this path and find a new one. It can be difficult and
scary, but not impossible. The forest around us is thick and
menacing, overgrown and mysterious. We don't know what's
out there. But the path is safe and familiar. Our instinct is to
stay on the path and be safe. But let's zoom out and take a look
at ourselves from a Google Earth point of view. From up in the
sky we can see ourselves as an ant sized speck moving slowly
along a path through the jungle. From this new vantage point
we can see the things around us that we can't see from down
there. We might see that our current path is headed towards a
dead end, or it might be headed towards a beautiful meadow.
There might be a pleasant oasis hidden alongside our path
that we never see. We might think we're all alone but in reality
right next to us are other people following their own paths,
never realizing we're all so close together.

From up here it would be great to be able to give ourselves
direction. To tell ourselves to take our machetes and hack
ourselves a new path just to the right, where we'll find a
wonderful new trail that's peaceful, paved, pleasant and invit-
ing. Or do the hard work to create a new trail to your left, and
our trail will connect with that of another person who we
would love to hike alongside with. Or decide to take a detour,
because the direction we're currently going in leads to a dead
end. Or stop for a minute and check our compass to confirm

our direction, because it turns out this whole time we've been going in circles. Unfortunately we'll never get this kind of guidance down here on the ground. We'll never know what lies ahead, or alongside, or around us in the jungle of life. It's up to us to explore, but many of us don't. Many of us go through life valuing the safety of the path more than the chance for greater happiness on an unknown path. But what if we choose to explore?

If we do choose to go off the path, to put in the hard work to hack through the jungle in search of some new way, we have to be prepared to fail. We might end up at a dead end, or looking over an impassable gorge, or even circle around to find ourselves back on the original path. I think it's worth the risk, though. Especially since the path we are on can get more and more unfriendly. It can become much harder to navigate as we go on, getting narrower, steeper, rockier, darker, more and more unpleasant. Sometimes this happens quickly and clearly, and sometimes this happens so slowly we don't immediately notice. Either way, often times we will find ourselves unhappy with our path in life, to the point where it becomes more desirable to blaze a trail into the jungle in search of a new path.

So grip your machete tightly and swing away at the jungle! This can mean changing careers, moving to a new place, ending a romantic relationship, starting a family, dying your hair, all those life events both big and small that can result in a new direction, in change. If things don't work out, take some time to go back to your original path and then strike out again. Or forget about the old path, and stumble along through the wilderness until you find another one. You can take your own advice now, imagining yourself looking down from above, knowing that somewhere in your future is a better path, a happier place. You might not be able to see it now, but it's out there somewhere, and you have the power to find it.

THIRTY-ONE

The Dirty Dishes of Doom

According to many studies, the most common thing couples fight about, after money and sex, is housework. You and your partner probably have different attitudes about what housework exactly is, what needs to be done, how it needs to be done, and who needs to do it. Those dishes aren't going to wash themselves!

Consider this scenario: You come home from work to the home you share with your partner. As you pass through the kitchen you see some dirty dishes sitting in the sink, dishes that your partner placed there without washing.

Do you react by:

A) washing the dishes and putting them away while whistling a happy tune?

OR

B) gritting your teeth as rage starts to burn deep down in the core of your being, your face getting flushed as you think about how inconsiderate and uncaring your partner is to commit this horribly selfish act?

If you said A, you have permission to skip this chapter. I envy you.

When we are in relationships, with all their opportunities for the exposure of deeply rooted feelings of anxiety, fear, and resentment, these emotions tend to manifest in innocuous, everyday ways. Little things like leaving the TV remote in the wrong place, not closing the bedroom door all the way, or leaving dirty dishes in the sink. Seemingly insignificant actions become loaded with deeper meaning. These objectively innocent occurrences become subjective affronts, triggers that inflame the deeper emotions beneath our surface.

What are these deeper feelings beneath the surface? That depends. These issues are going to be specific to your relationship. It could be a commitment issue, a lifestyle related problem, family conflict, disagreements regarding children, infidelity, intimacy issues, addiction, shame, or any number of issues many couples experience. But no matter what the specific, unique-to-your-own-relationship issues you're dealing with, the anger that wells up inside you when you see the Dirty Dishes of Doom in the sink is the same.

The deeper causes of this kind of relationship conflict often have their roots in our childhood experiences. Children whose parents addressed their physical and emotional needs in a supportive way, worked to develop a nurturing relationship, and took actions that instilled a sense of reliability tend to grow up to be adults who can replicate these qualities in their relationships. Children whose parents or caregivers did not engender a feeling of trust, who did not exhibit an appropriate amount of attention, and who acted out their own feelings of anger and anxiety in ways that confused the child tend to also replicate these qualities in their adult romantic relationships.

We've gone pretty deep here, starting with some dirty dishes in the sink and arriving at an analysis of our early childhood experiences, but it's important to realize that we are who we are because of everything that's happened to us since the day we were born, with the most formative experiences often happening earlier in our lives than most of us realize. In this relationship situation, are we aware that it isn't really the dishes we're angry about? Most of us aren't. Why doesn't he just wash the dishes? Why doesn't she just put them in the dishwasher? What's so hard about that? Why does this keep happening even though we've talked about it so many times? It's because we're unaware of how we're so influenced by our past experiences. The Dirty Dishes of Doom are the tip of the iceberg. Here we are, piloting our boat along the river of our relationship, and we keep bumping up against the tip of an iceberg, complaining about the tip of the iceberg, trying to avoid the tip of the iceberg, trying to come up with a plan to avoid the iceberg in the future, when in reality it's the rest of the iceberg hidden underwater that is the greatest danger.

So, how do we learn to better control the emotions guiding us in these moments? Well, you're already at step one: Awareness. The next step is to think more about why you get these flashes of anger when you see the dishes in the sink. Yes, you have talked about this before. Yes, your partner has said they'll try to clean the dishes. Yes, you felt good about talking about this and expressing your feelings. And yet, when you see those dishes all the rage flares up again.

What is this anger really about? That's where it gets specific to your situation, your relationship, your life. This is an area to explore with a therapist, either on your own or as a couple. Someone to guide you past the surface emotions and down into the deeper water. Because at this point, any more time you spend standing in the kitchen discussing the rules of the sink isn't going to help, and if it feels like it does, it's probably just a band aid. Band aids look nice, they make you feel like you've done something but they only heal scratches, not gaping wounds. And what we've got here is probably closer to a gaping wound.

So be aware of the Dirty Dishes of Doom and their impact on your emotional connection with your partner. Get deeper than the dishes and start to think about the rest of the iceberg beneath the surface. Find a therapist and explore how you might be acting out your childhood experiences in your current relationship. And while this process is taking place: maybe eat out more?

THIRTY-TWO

The Bridge of Pebbles

People often come to talk therapy because they have found themselves in a place in life they don't want to be. They feel stuck where they are and want to get moving towards somewhere else, but it seems hopeless. It's like they're standing on the bank of a river, and on the other side is the rest of their life, where the things they want to accomplish and hope to experience are waiting for them. The river is deep and the river is wide, but we can find a way across that river, using a metaphor.

We humans are always looking into the future. What should we do? What will make us happy? How will we ever achieve this that or the other? What if we fail? This can be paralyzing. Being in a career we don't like and wanting to change, or a relationship we are not happy in, we visualize ourselves feeling happy in a different situation, an alternative life to the one we're living right now. But it can be overwhelming to think about all the steps along the way to get to that situation. Not only can they be difficult and scary, but most of the time we have no idea what steps to take in order to get to where we want to be. That's when it's time to consider building a bridge of pebbles.

You can't build a bridge over the river in one fell swoop. It takes time and effort. Determination. Resilience. All demonstrated in small, incremental steps. Each of these little steps might seem hopeless by itself. It's like trying to lose weight. You can't just go to a four hour hot yoga class and lose twenty pounds. It takes small, incremental steps, and effort in different ways: going to the gym, eating healthier meals, drinking more water, getting enough sleep, bit by bit, over time, to get to the place you want to be.

These small steps are the pebbles. When you toss that first pebble into the river, it won't look like anything has changed. The water's still rushing by. There's still no path across the river, but don't get discouraged! Actually, scratch that: it's fine if you get discouraged. It's totally expected actually. Get discouraged! But don't give up. Toss that next pebble in the river. And the next one. Keep tossing those pebbles.

Eventually you'll see a mound of pebbles grow into a stepping stone. A first step along what will eventually be a bridge to the life you want to live. Depending on your situation this could take weeks, months, even years. But during this time you're not solely focused on the bridge. You're living your life! You're waking up, eating, working, living, loving, going to bed, waking up, repeating. And each day you're tossing pebbles into that river. If you keep at it, one day you'll find yourself standing closer to the other side of the river. Now you're creating some momentum! You can feel good about yourself, proud of what you've accomplished so far. You've come far enough to be able to look back at where you came from. You're closer to where you want to be.

It should get easier once you start to see results, which is a great motivator. Keep working at it, and eventually you'll get to the other side. Or rather, you'll find yourself on the other side. It might surprise you, actually. It happened so slowly you didn't notice right away. Now you can look back at this pebble bridge you built and know that it's constructed of the many single little pebbles you threw in there. Every time you went to the gym, every date you went on that turned out to be lame, every work contact you called to pick their brain about switching careers, every little pebble that didn't seem significant on its own have combined to get you to where you are today. The bridge to where we want to be in life is built from the many small steps we take towards getting there.

THIRTY-THREE

Programming Your Life Macro

M*acro* is short for *macroinstruction*. A macroinstruction is a programmable pattern that takes a series of instructions and executes them in a sequence after a single keystroke. We use macros every time we hit Command-C to copy and Command-V to paste, when we Shift-Command-Control-Tab whatever. In fact, I just used a macro to move this whole paragraph here from a completely different file. I don't remember when exactly I realized I could use a keyboard shortcut instead of the mouse hovering up in the menu bar and clicking in three or four steps, but I can't imagine not doing it now. In the same way, we can program our own life macros as we become more aware of our own cycles of behavior, and use them to shorten the time spent fighting or crying or in conflict and increase the time we feel like we're actually enjoying life. Eventually we'll look back on how long it took us to do things before we started using the macro.

Part of the work of talk therapy is guiding clients to

examine their actions and develop an understanding of their own cycles of shame or anger or addiction or passive aggressiveness or whatever they're experiencing. As we work together, they will begin to be able to identify these patterns and analyze how they happen, why they happen, and if they want to stop them from happening. A good example is a client talking about a fight they had with their partner. This might include a description of the setting, the background, the incident, the reaction, the aftermath, and the reconciliation. The client sees it all happening with a new sense of awareness, and understands how this pattern has directed their lives for as long as it has. And after the client sees the cycle, they ask how they can break the cycle.

Let's not think about it in terms of breaking the cycle. Let's think about it like we're programming an emotional macroinstruction sequence. We've identified all the steps we want to be in this sequence: setting, background, incident, reaction, aftermath, reconciliation. We know we're going to go through these stages, and instead of figuring out how to stop these stages from happening, we will learn to shrink the time it takes to experience them.

But how do we accomplish this? We talk about it. We come into session with stories from the previous week about how we struggled with something and analyze what happened and how we felt about it. We talk about the difference between what happened objectively and how we reacted to it subjectively. We observe whether we felt like we were powerless to stop acting the way we were, or if we were able to change how we felt or reacted, even if just a little bit. This is what people mean when they refer to "doing the work". It's about having the courage to talk about things that are scary and painful that we've spent a long time avoiding talking about.

Every session we spend doing the work the reaction time between conflict and resolution shrinks. This is how we program our own emotional life macros. You know what triggers you, you know how you react, you know the reasons why, you know how you would rather react, and you know you have the power to act and feel differently. This work will help to shrink the time between conflict and resolution from a week to day to a couple of hours and hopefully to the point where it all happens instantly in our minds. This cycle to emotional reactions will eventually be accomplished in the stroke of a key, enabling us to skip through the bad stuff and enjoy the good stuff. Shift-Command-PersonalGrowth-Happiness!

THIRTY-FOUR

Meditate With Me

Meditation is a topic that comes up often in therapy. It's a great way to address anxiety and help clients learn to be more aware of the moment they are in, instead of worrying about what will happen in the future to the detriment of their experience in the present. It can be intimidating, however, and unfamiliar in a way that makes it difficult to engage in for some people. I am by no means a Zen monk of meditation knowledge or experience, but I have developed my own practice over the years, and I share my experience with clients who I think would benefit from it.

Before I started meditating it seemed like a mysterious process. I pictured Zen monks sitting cross legged in silence, experiencing some kind of magical calmness I could only hope to attain. Then I started meditating, and you will not be surprised to hear that my experience was anything but monk-like. I could barely sit still for five minutes as my mind raced with thoughts of to-do lists and past and future grievances, mostly imagined. My foot would fall asleep and I would question how I was sitting, where I was sitting, and how long I was sitting for, all at the same time. I wanted to skip the times I had assigned myself to meditate, and then I felt guilty for wanting to skip them. From the outside meditation looked easy, but from the inside it was a whole different story. It's like the sausage factory expression, reflecting on how the experience of eating a sausage can be so different from seeing how it actually gets made. I think about how from the outside I must look very much at peace when I meditate, while on the inside my mind is furiously making sausages.

At first I wanted to learn how to meditate the "right way", but eventually I realized this wasn't going to happen because there is no "right way". There is only the way that works best for us each as individuals. So I stuck with it. And it was a long, slow process, with numerous stops and starts, but eventually I found a practice that worked for me. Part of the reason I was able to reach this point was that I learned to accept what I had previously seen as flaws in the process. Now, when my mind races or my foot falls asleep or I skip a session I don't let myself feel bad about it. I accept it as a part of the practice. I remind myself that I wouldn't expect myself to be able to run a marathon without any training. I would have to start slowly, running a little bit more each day until I reached my goal. Same thing with meditation. It's a process, not a goal.

In that spirit I want to share with you what's going on in my head when I meditate. I sat for a 5 minute session and tried to dictate every thought that came up. It certainly made for an atypical meditation experience, but I think you'll see just how different it can look from the outside versus the inside.

BEGIN MEDITATION SESSION

Okay, I just set the timer for five minutes, breath deep through the nose, sit up straight, shoulders back… And now noticing all the sounds around me. I can hear cars driving by across the street. Coming and going. Now the birds chirping outside. Wow, lots of different birds right now. And a car alarm very faintly I think. Probably not one of the neighbors. Maybe parked a few streets over, across from the—

Okay, let's refocus, breath deep, exhale, sit up straight. Picturing a white sandy beach with a blue ocean, maybe a wicker chair and I'm wearing a straw hat. Drinking a beer. Wait, why am I picturing this? I never do that. Gotta think about something else. Actually let's try not to think about anything else…

Breath deep, exhale, sit up straight. Unclench the jaw, feel the face relax. It's amazing how much tension I carry in my jaw. It's no wonder I grind my teeth. Good thing I got that mouthguard to sleep with at night. Gotta take care of my teeth. I should have flossed this morning. That's all I need are cavities. But it's a been a while since my last one. When did I even have my last cavity?

Okay, breath deep, sit up straight. Sit in silence. Listen for the silence. There it is. A quiet moment. Now I hear the ticking of the clock. Can't believe it's been ticking this whole time and I'm just now noticing it. I never hear it when I'm sitting at my desk. God my shoulders are hunched. My posture is horrible at the computer. I should get a standing desk. But they're expensive. That's all I need it is to spend more money. I still have to pay my Amex bill…

Okay, breath deep, sit up straight. Unclench the jaw. Let the jaw hang. God, my eyebrows are so furrowed! Relax the eyebrows too, the whole face. Just let everything relax. No wonder I'm getting wrinkles, I go around all day with my face all tensed up. Would it even be possible to walk around with a fully relaxed face? I'd probably look like I had plastic surgery or something—

Breath deep through the nose, exhale, shoulders back. Sit up straight. Sounds like a truck pulling up outside. Could be Amazon. Hope they don't leave a delivery for me at the foot of the steps. Could get stolen. Always concerned about that. Did I even order anything from Amazon lately? I did buy some sandals for my daughter on Zappos. But she probably won't like them so I'll have to return them, print up the shipping label, order another pair—

Okay, breath deep, sit up straight. Relax the face. Just sit. Breath and sit. Birds are still tweeting. Ha, I almost said twerking. So many bad twerking videos on Tik Tok. Which my daughter is on all the time. Hope she's not learning to twerk. Should I have a talk with her about that? How do you have twerk talk? She's be mortified to even hear me say the word twerk.

Alright, breath deep, relax, shoulders back. Enjoy the silence. Ah, there's the ticking clock. There must be so much noise in my mind for me to not hear it. Follow the ticking clock. Everything else right now is silent. How could I ever not hear it? How noisy is it in my mind that I can't hear the tick?

Breath deep, through the nose, sit up straight, relax the face. Quiet. Sound of a skateboard rolling down the sidewalk outside. I wanted to be a skater so bad when I was a kid but I was horrible at it. Now if I got on a skateboard I'd probably fall and break my wrist. Then I'd have to go to the hospital and deal with all the insurance. Am I on a good plan right now? I bet I'm spending too much money. And it's expensive!

Stop. Breath deep, through the nose, sit up straight, relax the face. Maybe I'll count the ticks of the clock. 1, 2,3,4,5,6... Lots of birds tweeting now. Should I put that hummingbird feeder back up? The one my mom got me. It's such a cheaply made thing but she'd like for me to use it. But I don't want to. Is that bad?

Whoa, okay, breath deep, through the nose, sit up straight, relax the face. My head itches now. Don't scratch it. Don't move. Ignore it and it'll go away. But it's not. Starting to tingle. Okay, one quick scratch, then back to the breath.

Breath deep, through the nose, sit up straight, relax the face. And of course now that spot I scratched is getting even more itchy. Come on, we can ignore that. Let's focus on the breath. Breathe one two three, exhale one two three. Sit. Breathe one two three, exhale one two three. When I transcribe this am I going to write out the numbers one two three, or am I going to use the number symbols 1 2 3? Write them out I think. Numbers might look weird with punctuation.

Stop. Breath deep, through the nose, sit up straight, relax the face. And there's another itch in the same spot. I should be able to ignore it and it will go away. The itch is all in my mind.

But what if there's a bug on me? What if a mosquito is just about to bite me? Come on, there aren't any mosquitos around here. But it could be some other insect. Something crawling on my skin at this very moment—

Okay, another deep breath through the nose. Hold it a little bit longer, then exhale. And quiet. A moment between traffic when there are no car sounds. That's a nice moment. And there's the ticking clock. Yeah, this moment feels good. It's funny how I can sit here for so long and only feel like I'm really in the moment every so— (TIMER GOES OFF) Woo hoo, finished!

END MEDITATION SESSION

When the timer goes off my eyes pop open instantly. I'm always a little surprised by the sound, and then by the fact that I was able to make it through the whole session. I usually try to sit for twenty minutes, a number that I've worked up to, starting out with five. Sometimes I'll cut a session short if I feel like it. I try not to feel guilty about this. And it feels good to give myself permission if I don't feel like it. But most of the time I'm able to sit for a whole session.

Reading over this transcript it certainly doesn't seem like a peaceful, tranquil experience. However, it didn't feel as chaotic in my mind as it looks on the page. In between all of the runaway thoughts there are moments of peace and clarity. Brief moments, usually after a deep breath and an exhale, where I felt like how I would imagine those Zen Japanese monks feel. The rest of the time was spent reeling in those runaway thoughts. Which, as I read it now, looks like it must feel repetitive and frustrating. It doesn't feel that way when I'm doing it, though. That time spent chasing runaway thoughts wasn't something to avoid, something to strive to eliminate. That time is the whole point. It's the mental workout, the training of my brain to stop leaping backwards or forwards in time, and be here in the moment. Think about this if you're considering starting your own meditation practice. There's no wrong way to do it. There's only the way that works best for you, which takes time and effort to discover.

THIRTY-FIVE

The Poker Game of Life

C lients I work with regarding anxiety sometimes tend to overanalyze the decisions they make in life, most of the time in a negative light. They might have a decision to make regarding a job opportunity, or a choice about a romantic relationship, or some other important option that has the potential to change their lives in a big way. If the choice they make turns out badly, they excoriate themselves, reinforcing the image they have about themselves as making poor choices, doing the wrong thing, having things always turn out badly in the end.

This reminds me of a concept that is often applied in the game of poker called "results oriented thinking". If the client plays poker I might describe it in a more detailed way. If they do not I will just sketch out the general idea. The concept of results oriented thinking refers to the tendency for us humans to decide whether or not we made the right decision based on the outcome of our decision. However, this approach minimizes one of the most important factors affecting the results of our decisions: Chance. Luck. Fate. Whatever you want to call it, sometimes the most important factors affecting the decisions we make in life are out of our control. So what can we control? Only the things we take into consideration before we make our decision.

Let's say a client has a choice between job offers at two different companies. They analyze their options, make a list of pros and cons, consider the possible future outcomes as best they can, and then make a decision. Two months later one of the companies file for bankruptcy and goes out of business. The other company is bought by a larger company and flourishes. Two completely different scenarios.

If this client chose the job at the company that ends up flourishing, they'd probably feel like they made the right decision. If they chose the job at the company that went bankrupt, they'd most likely feel like they made the wrong decision. The truth, however, is that they made the best decision they could with the information they had at the time. Not a good or bad decision, but the best one. This relates to poker in the sense that logic and rational decisions affect your ability to win, but ultimately there is a certain amount of luck involved that is out of our control. You might have a 99% chance to win a hand based on a decision you made to put all your chips into the middle. You've made the best choice you can. If that 1% outcome happens though, and you lose all your chips, of course you're going go feel bad about it. But are you going to wish you made a different decision? You certainly would if you could go back in time knowing what you know now about how the hand turned out. But that's impossible! And the irony is that we often treat ourselves as if we should have known what was going to happen. That is where much of the anxiety and regret we feel about choices that turn out badly come from. We are essentially giving ourselves a hard time for not being able to predict the future!

Positive outcomes make it easy to think we did everything right. Negative outcomes make it easy to think we did everything wrong. The results are what counts, right? Well, certainly the results are important, but we're setting ourselves up for disaster if we consider only the results when assessing our choices. If we prepare for a decision without much effort or care but still succeed, what lesson will we take from this? That what little we did to prepare last time was enough to succeed, and we can approach the next decision with the same attitude and expect things to work out well again. If we prepare well but fail, what lesson will we take from that? That we're not able to do the thing we tried to do, even though we put so much work into it, so why bother trying our best again if we failed last time?

We can only do our best. If we put in the work, the effort, and the energy, then we have done all we can. If it doesn't work out, we can't let that dictate how we approach things in the future. We can't be afraid to fail, and we can't get lulled into complacency by success. Do your best in preparation, and if you win, great! If you don't, be confident that you'll get lucky the next time. In the poker game of life there is a lot you can control, but more that you can't. Keep playing the game as best you can, making the best decisions you can with the information you have at the time, and eventually you'll be the one stacking all the chips.

THIRTY-SIX

The Rising Waters of Change

C hange is one of the most commons topics discussed in
talk therapy. Whether it's the end of a relationship, the
death of a loved one, economic challenges, medical issues, or a
natural disaster, the adjustment of having to go from the way
things were to the way things are is a common source of stress.
There's even a clinical diagnosis for this: Adjustment Disorder
(that's 309.0, with various F-code specifiers related to symptoms like depression or anxiety, for all you Diagnostic and
Statistical Manual of Mental Disorder fans out there).

We know change is hard. We don't like to change. It's not
in our nature as human beings. We're evolutionarily
programmed to avoid change, going all the way back to when
our ancestors huddled in dark caves, happy to be relatively safe
from the mystery and danger outside. However, eventually
there was one intrepid soul among them who wanted more,
who thought he could do better, who felt like there was a
brighter future out there outside the cave. So he ventured out

into the unknown. What happened to him? Nobody knows! He could have found a great new cave in a much nicer neighborhood, or he could have been eaten by something big and furry with sharp teeth. The rest of the cavemen were left to pass their status quo loving, safety seeking, change avoiding genes down to future generations.

Even though it's been thousands of years since those early humans huddled around a fire, ruled by the difference between the warmth and safety of home versus the dark scary mystery of "out there", we still carry in our DNA some of the survival mechanisms developed by our ancestors. Here we focus on the Fight or Flight response. This examines the feelings we have when confronted with a threat: Do we confront it or do we run away? These feelings trigger a reaction not just mentally but physically as well. Where in ancient times this response might have been triggered by an encounter with a saber toothed tiger, today it might be triggered by the loss of a job, or the end of a romantic relationship. This response can include an increased heart rate, rapid breathing, pale or flushed skin, and muscle tension or trembling. We truly feel it in our body. But where the caveman seeing the saber toothed tiger might be a one time event that ends after that encounter, in our modern world we might feel this kind of physical reaction every time we see our ex-partner's furniture they left when they moved out, or hear that song we remember them doing at karaoke the night we met. Where our ancestors experienced the Fight or Flight response when venturing outside the cave, gathering food in the presence of possible predators, in this modern world we are continuously bombarded by stimuli that can trigger us. With all our advanced technology and social media options we are now able to bombard ourselves constantly with stimuli that can cause this feeling. Instead of an encounter with an actual saber toothed tiger, it's the Instagram account @saber_toothedtiger99.

How is this aversion to change represented in this modern world? Instead of leaving the safety of the cave, it's leaving the job or the relationship, the situations we find ourselves in where we might not be happy but consider things more desirable than venturing out into the unknown. A job in a career that's not fulfilling provides a steady paycheck, job security, insurance, all things we value. But if we complain all the time about how unfulfilling it is and how miserable we are, what keeps us from quitting and trying to find something else? The fear of change. A relationship we've been in for a long time might feel like a dead end. We might complain that we've hit a rough patch, our momentum is stalled, our relationship isn't progressing. But should we break up? Hell no, I don't want to be single again! Maybe my partner really is "the one" and I just haven't come around to accepting it. Maybe I just need to adjust my expectations. Maybe the problem is me. Sound familiar?

The positive aspects of our situation outweigh the negative aspects, but only until they don't. In this scenario, negative feelings of unhappiness and dissatisfaction are represented by a body of rising water, and our resistance to change is a dam of denial that we've built to hold that water back. We stand on the top of the dam and look down at the water as it slowly rises, knowing that it will eventually reach the top of the dam, but we deny this eventuality. Why do we do this? Because we're not yet ready to change. We decide it's better to wait it out rather than take a leap into the unknown. It's a constant battle to judge the pros and cons of each course of action, and this battle is a consistent source of stress and anxiety.

Over the course of our lives we build this dam brick by brick, thought by thought, reason by reason, emotion by emotion. Over time, the water rises. Nothing can stop the water from rising. Some of us keep building this dam for our entire lives, always one step ahead of the water. For some of us the water eventually reaches the top of the dam and flows over, forcing us into action, driving us to confront the change. Only when we feel like something has "clicked" inside us emotionally, like a switch has finally flipped, do we finally feel it's worth it to quit that job, to end that relationship, to make that difficult decision.

You'll know if you've been through this process when, after the water flows over your dam and forces you into action and you make a decision and things change, one day you wake up and look in the mirror and realize you are happier and say to yourself "I wish I'd made that decision a lot sooner!". Well, the irony here is that you're not capable of making that change, no matter how much you intellectually understand the reasons for doing it, until you're emotionally ready. No amount of debate or reasoning or therapy or other people telling you they did it and you can too will convince your emotions to feel differently until they're ready to. Knowing the water will only continue to rise isn't always enough to make us take action. We need the cold reality of wet feet to motivate us to take those first steps down a new path.

Even though many of us may find ourselves sharing the similarities of this type of situation, our specifics are unique.

Some of our dams are higher than others. Some of our water rises faster than others. Some of us have one big dam, while others have a complicated interlocking series of dams. Much of the unhappiness people feel in the course of their everyday lives about this is related to the guilt they feel about not acting when intellectually they know change would be better for them. It's bad enough to be in a situation that makes you unhappy, or at least does not provide much happiness. We tend to make this worse by then giving ourselves a hard time for not doing anything about it. My advice to you when you find yourself in this situation is to let yourself feel these feelings without beating yourself up. Eventually at some point your emotions will catch up to your conscious thoughts, and you'll find yourself ready to act. The water of change will eventually rise above your dam of denial, getting your metaphorical feet wet, and wet feet are often the final motivation we need to leave behind an undesirable past and embrace an uncertain future.

THIRTY-SEVEN

The Falling Leaf

Mindfulness is a great way to reduce anxiety and stress. Many people think only of meditation when they consider mindfulness, but there are a multitude of ways to experience it. There are familiar ways, like yoga or exercise, but once you appreciate what mindfulness really means you can find it in any activity. By focussing on the moment at hand, we can learn to practice not worrying so much about the future or regretting the past, and appreciate our lives in the present moment. It also engenders a sense of self acceptance and a suspension of judgement that can help us be kinder to ourselves and to others. There are many established ways to practice mindfulness, but there is no rule that says you can only experience it in certain ways. I find that when I'm more in touch with this feeling of mindfulness, I tend to find moments in my everyday life that reflect it, and I try to recognize and appreciate those moments. One of my favorite ways to experience mindfulness in everyday life is by catching a falling leaf.

I spend lots of time walking in my neighborhood, getting exercise and sunshine, listening to podcasts or talking on the phone. One time I was walking along and noticed a tall tree with leaves that were starting to change color from green to yellow and brown. Just then a gust of wind blew a leaf off a limb. As it started to flutter to the ground my first instinct was to run and catch it, but then I decided not to, and then I changed my mind just as fast and wanted to catch it, but before I could move the wind picked up and delivered the leaf right to me. All I had to do was hold out my hand and catch it. I guess I was in an especially pensive mood that day, because as I held the leaf I thought about how long it had been on that tree, how many days it must have taken to slowly grow and mature and get to the point where it was ready to fall, and the many gusts of wind that came closer and closer to dislodging it, until finally at some random moment its time had come, and the leaf fell down to me, who had spent my life traveling to arrive here at the exact moment the leaf fell.

I took the leaf home and put it on my desk. When I looked at it it reminded me of how my entire life and that leaf's entire life had built up to one serendipitous moment when we crossed paths. I also appreciated that I could easily not have seen the leaf fall and continued walking. What would have happened then? Nothing, I guess. The leaf would have fluttered to the ground, and nobody would have noticed. In fact, moments like that happen millions of times a day. Every leaf on a tree has to fall eventually. I just happened to be there and noticed it happening.

The mindfulness aspect I took away from this experience was how much I enjoy seeing these moments happen. Looking for falling leaves while I'm walking means I'm aware of my surroundings, not walking along trapped in anxious thoughts about the to-do list of the future. It made me more aware of the color of the sky and the feeling of the breeze on my skin, as opposed to self critical thoughts about difficult relationships from the past and how they might pop up again in the future. It's easy to walk along, head down, full of thoughts about everything except what's happening right around you. Looking for falling leaves on my walks unlocked a mindfulness practice that I find simple and effective.

Here's the thing about falling leaves, though: They're not easy to catch! Those things flutter like a knuckleball. There are also obstacles to consider, curbs to avoid tripping over, streets to avoid darting into while your eyes are locked in on a falling leaf. It got to the point where my walks were getting longer because I was spending too much time standing under trees waiting for a leaf to fall. I think the universe was teasing me by making the first time I caught a falling leaf so easy. So the next time you notice a leaf falling from a tree, stop and consider it. Maybe try to catch it. But be prepared to experience how hard it is to catch a falling leaf. Much like being in the moment, it sounds simple but it's not as easy as you think.

THIRTY-EIGHT

Anger = Electricity

Anger is a source of and reaction to many of the issues people come to therapy for. When I work with clients about issues involving anger, we often examine their own emotional history and the ways in which it contains the fuel that their anger feeds on in the present. This usually involves childhood experiences with their parents, emotional or physical trauma they have experienced, and many other factors. A great deal of personal growth and awareness can be realized as a result of this introspection, but that isn't always what the client wants to talk about when they're in a session with me discussing something that got them really angry. What they want to talk about is their anger! And how they reacted to it, how the people around them reacted to it, and whether or not they want to try to learn to react differently. They may want to learn how to not react with such anger. Or they might not yet be aware of themselves as the source of this anger, and instead want help getting other people to stop making them angry.

Either way, for them it's all about dealing with anger in the moment.

We're in a situation and something happens that makes us angry. We feel it start to well up inside us. Blood rushes to our head. We clench our jaws. We ball our fists. We want to say something mean. Or yell. Or be passive aggressive. We might feel like we're bottling up the anger but it's coming out in our tone of voice and the tension in our bodies. The anger has arrived, and we're going to let the people we're with know we're angry. We're going to show them, one way or another. The anger has to come out somehow, right? Absolutely. Better to let the anger out than suppress it, because that only means it will come out later on in a different way and maybe even more intensely. But I think we can learn to let the anger out in a safer way. A way that doesn't hurt the people around us. In this case, I think of anger like electricity.

I'm no electricity-ologist, but I did a bunch of Googling and have a general understanding of how it works. Suffice to say, electricity is a powerful force and you can get hurt very badly if you are electrocuted. But with so many uses for electricity in our modern world and the multitude of ways we interact with it, how do we avoid getting hurt? Well, there's a concept called *grounding,* which is when instead of you touching something electric and getting shocked, the flow of electricity is directed into the ground, where it dissipates safely. For purposes of this chapter, electricity can either flow out of you and cause you or the people around you pain, or it can flow through you and become grounded and dissipate safely.

Anger and electricity are similar in this way. Electricity, like water, follows the path of least resistance. Anger does too, and that path often leads to our mouth, where it emerges as yelling and mean words. But how can we learn to ground ourselves and avoid the pain of anger? I like to visualize this anger flowing through us and away in the same way that electricity might flow through us and then through a grounding device and away from us. How can we ground our anger? Different ways. It might come from an increased awareness of why we're angry. Understanding we're about to be put in a situation where we might get angry, and then feel that anger, and then know that we don't want to direct that anger to the people around us. Just going through the process of thinking about it can help ground the anger. Another grounding tactic is to stop when we feel the anger coming up and close our eyes, breath deeply, and count to ten. Sometimes we can ground our anger if we engage in some self-talk and challenge ourselves to verbalize why we're angry, and by putting it into words the anger becomes grounded. Another technique is more somatic (related to the body), and this involves putting your hand down on a table or some other surface and visualizing your anger flowing through you and into the table and down into the ground. You're grounding yourself, letting the anger pass through you harmlessly the same way electricity might. Instead of coming out of your mouth and hurting people it flows out of your body a different way, a way that renders it harmless.

Anger and electricity are both powerful forces that can hurt us and the people around us if we're not equipped with the proper safety precautions. Scientists have studied electricity and made great strides in learning to harness its energy to do great things, while at the same time making it safe to use. Scientists have not studied anger and have not learned how to harness the power of anger to do great things while making it safe to use (although Bruce Banner keeps trying). It's up to us to try find our own way to manage our anger so it doesn't cause us and the people around us pain and suffering. For many of of us being angry feels good, and the struggle is to forego this good feeling and instead let the anger flow through us without acting on it.

THIRTY-NINE

Everyone Needs a Good Mechanic

There is a renewed interest in mental health in our society nowadays, with a growing appreciation for talk therapy. Zoom and other networking technologies, combined with the potential for increased engagement via social media, have made therapy accessible to people who might not have considered it before. For those who have never experienced talk therapy, and who are considering reaching out for the first time but unsure of what to expect, I like to compare the process of seeing a therapist to something most of us can relate to: seeing a mechanic.

We all know how important cars are in our everyday lives, but we usually appreciate them the most when they break down. It can be the same way with therapy. Most people get along fine in their everyday lives until they encounter some crisis that sends them into a spiral of depression or anxiety and motivates them to reach out for help. This leads to a wonderful analogy: Mechanic is to car as therapist is to mind. It might start with you cruising along through life, seemingly with no worries. Things are going well, until one day your car starts making a horrible squeaking noise. You really don't want to deal with going to the mechanic (therapist) though, so you soldier on and ignore it and hope it goes away. But it doesn't. In fact, it gets worse. So you finally do some research, find a mechanic (therapist) that people seem to like, maybe a referral from a trusted friend, and you schedule an appointment.

You arrive at this appointment with an idea of what the problem is. You tell the mechanic (therapist) that there must be something wrong with the engine because this noise happens whenever you press the gas. If he could just fix the engine as quickly and cheaply as possible you'll be on your merry way. But the mechanic (therapist), after hearing this diagnosis of yours, tells you he needs to know more about your car (personal history) and wants to run a full diagnostic exam and check everything out to identify the true source of the problem. You tell the mechanic (therapist) you're pretty sure you know what the problem is, but if he needs to do some more tests then fine, go ahead. You know it's a good idea to get the whole car checked out, that there might be bigger issues lurking beneath the surface here, but you don't want him to find anything else wrong, because you're not interested in dealing with any more problems other than what you already know about with your car (life). However, deep down inside you have a sneaking suspicion there might be a bigger problem. Maybe something related to the time you hit a curb driving home from dinner a few months back (a recent breakup with a romanic partner or clash with a family member). You're just hoping the mechanic (therapist) doesn't find anything and you get the all clear to resume your life as currently constructed.

Your mechanic runs a diagnostic exam and then sits down with you to share his findings. It turns out your fuel filters are clogged, your catalytic converter is dying, and there's a dent in the front left axle which looks like it happened as a result of some jarring movement that might have happened in a previous accident. Was there any unspoken accident (personal trauma) in your past you neglected to tell the mechanic (therapist) about? Yes, you admit, you did accidentally drive up on a curb a few months ago. It was a traumatic accident (like job loss, a divorce, a death) but the car still drove fine after that. It didn't seem like that big a deal, that's why you didn't mention it.

So the mechanic (therapist) gives you his opinion. You have some maintenance related problems to fix (anger issues, passive aggressive behavior, relationship struggles), but there's also a bigger problem regarding the inner workings of your car (unaddressed childhood trauma, repressed anger, addiction issues). He can address the smaller problems with a short term solution, but that won't help the deeper problem. To fix that will take more time, and it might even uncover further problems in the process, but in the long run your car (life) will run much better for all this work.

You were hoping it wouldn't come to this. You didn't want the mechanic (therapist) to find the problem that you knew in your heart to be the true cause of your issues. It would be very easy to turn down the mechanic's (therapist's) offer to work on the problem with you. You could just not come back and continue to drive your car with the annoying squeaky sound until it <u>really</u> becomes a problem, but who knows when that might be. You don't want to deal with making an appointment to put your car in the shop and getting a rental car during the time the work is being done. But you know that if you avoid addressing this problem, every day you'll get in your car knowing there's something wrong with it, and this will bother you. This knowledge will gnaw at you and make your life less enjoyable as you continue to drive this damaged car, and you also know that as you continue to drive it without addressing the problem you'll only be making it worse.

So you decide to suck it up and go with the mechanic's (therapist's) recommendation. You'll get the work done. So you schedule the necessary appointments with your mechanic (therapist), putting your trust in him to do a good job. But then, just as you feared, he gets in there under the hood and finds a couple more problems, things you never knew about. You have a fuel line leak (growing addiction issue), the tires are beginning to lose their tread (low level depression), and a crucial engine gasket is about to blow because it was installed incorrectly and threatens to spray oil all over the chassis (an unresolved issue with your father is driving you to act out in ways that negatively affect your current relationship). You shake your head, feeling down because you've found all these things wrong with your car (yourself), but the mechanic (thera-pist) is there to tell you it's not your fault. He sees cars (people) with issues like this all the time, and he knows that after doing all the necessary repairs (therapy sessions) you'll be better than ever.

So the works continues. It takes some time, but eventually it gets done. When you finally pick up your car the mechanic (therapist) tells you it's good to go, but he makes it clear you need to keep up with your scheduled maintenance (mindfulness practice, regular therapy), lest you encounter the same problems again. You smile and thank him, feeling better now that you have addressed the underlying issues that were the true cause of your car's (emotional) troubles. Your car now feels familiar yet new at the same time. It looks the same but it drives better. You pull out of the mechanic's parking lot (therapist's office) with a smile on your face, ready to continue your drive down the road (of life) with the knowledge that you've done the proper work on your car (self) to help get you where you need to go without breaking down (breaking down). Enjoy the changes you've made, and drive safe!

FORTY

The Results of Meditation

The practice of meditation is a great way for clients to become more aware of the power of their own minds in determining how they feel and act. This can take the shape of a wide range of activities, from twice daily twenty minute silent meditation sessions to just going for a walk. Different clients respond to different approaches, but one thing they all have in common is a desire to eventually see how their meditation practice positively affects their real lives. One client in particular was a new parent, and wanted to make sure he wasn't preoccupied with work thoughts when he was with his child. He said he wanted to make sure to be "in the moment" as a parent. He understood how his meditation practice was supposed to help him do this in theory. He just hadn't yet seen something that he could point to in his interactions with his family as something he was doing or feeling differently as a result of meditating. He wanted to know when he would be able to spot these kind of changes. He wanted to see the results!

This led to an interesting discussion. How does learning to meditate help us in real life? How does being more in touch with the moment affect us on a day to day basis in a tangible, noticeable way? How does learning how to wax a car prepare us to compete in the All-Valley Karate Championships? First of all, I remind clients that they don't have to change what they're doing or try any harder. The fact that we're having this conversation means we're on the right path. Now that we're talking about this specific issue, I encourage clients to keep their emotional eyes open over the coming weeks, looking for evidence of a change in their behavior or attitude in the moment that was influenced by their mindfulness practice. Something to confirm what we suspect about how our lives seem calmer or different in a positive way, but we just can't put on finger on a specific moment. And then I share a moment of my own.

I had just started meditating, mainly to help manage the stress related to my writing career. I wasn't working as much as I wanted to, and not on projects I enjoyed working on. I was in the process of reconnecting with people I'd worked with in the past. I ended up emailing an actor I had worked with on a previous project, and he invited me to come down to visit him on the set of his latest show. I went down to the set, and the actor's assistant found me and led me to his dressing room. The actor had twenty minutes until he was needed on set, and we could hang out and chat until then. And so we did. It was pleasant, and I was doing a good job of balancing the part of myself that was talking about my recent projects and catching up on his with the part of myself that felt nervous, uncomfort-able, and like I didn't belong here. I didn't want to come off as needy, but I still wanted this actor to know I was available for future staff or development work, and I thought I was doing a good job of communicating that. I remember checking the time and seeing it had been about twenty minutes, and feeling relieved because it felt like by that point I had nothing left to talk about. Just then the assistant poked his head in and informed us that it would be another thirty minutes until he was needed on set. The actor said that was fine, and welcomed me to hang out till then. Here's where I noticed the mindful-ness practice kicking in.

My first instinct was to run. Like the feeling when you've been at a party for awhile and don't know anyone and you feel awkward and want to make a quick exit. I projected my inse-curities onto the actor and reasoned out why I should leave. Certainly I'm imposing on him, he'd prefer for me to leave anyways, he's so busy and here I am talking about me, I should just get out of here now before I say anything embarrassing. In the past I would have run with these feelings and acted on them. I would have gone into auto pilot and found myself making an excuse to leave and heading towards my car. However, in this moment I didn't do that. Instead, I gave those anxious feelings a chance to flow through me without acting on them. I just observed them. Here I am, feeling needy and ashamed and awkward and wishing I wasn't here. I'm going to feel these feelings but I'm not going to act on them. I'm just going to sit with them for a moment. And then, after that moment, those feelings were gone. And after that moment I looked up at the actor and said sure, I'd love to hang a little more, no problem. Mind you, all of this took less than a second. But it was all the thinking I had put into the process that made it work so quickly.

We ended up having a great talk about topics I never considered. I felt more comfortable and relaxed. It didn't feel like I was imposing on him or that he was wishing I would leave. I realized those fears were manufactured in my mind, and not based in reality. After a while the assistant popped back in and said they were ready on the set so we went down there, where the actor introduced me to the writing staff and I got to say hi to some crew members I knew. I watched a couple of takes and then left when they were done shooting. As I drove home I thought about how in the past I would have grasped that moment of doubt and insecurity and used it to escape, to avoid the risk of embarrassment or shame. I could see how my meditation practice helped me stop and identify these feelings and observe them without acting on them. This led me to change how I approached the moment in real life for the better, and I could see clearly how this approach was influenced by my meditation practice. TLDR: Meditation: It really works!

FORTY-ONE

The Unsent Letter

There are many tools in the therapist's tool box to use as they work with clients. One of them is particularly effective when working with a client who has unresolved issues with their parents. Sometimes we don't fully appreciate the effects our early childhood experiences regarding our parents have on the rest of our lives. In talk therapy we might find ourselves thinking for the first time about how the things our parents did and said might be causes of the issues that have brought us to therapy. It can be an emotional experience to relate as an adult to the way our parents acted towards us when we were children. One way to help process these emotions is to write our parents a letter.

Here's how it works: The client sits down to write a letter to a parent. What is the content of this letter? The content is all the things we're starting to realize about our childhood and how it affects us today. It is the realizations and fears and unacknowledged feelings and events that have been left unsaid over the years. It's the pain and trauma that we have glossed over, made excuses for, rationalized, even the small things that we minimized but which might have had a stronger emotional impact than we thought. Maybe your parents were absent from your life when you needed them the most. Maybe they dealt with addiction issues that you couldn't understand at the time. Perhaps a divorce caused a great deal of unresolved emotional trauma at an early age. But let's not minimize the fact that even without an identifiable traumatic event or pattern like divorce or addiction we can still have experienced traumatic childhood events in the course of what we might consider our normal daily lives growing up. We each have our own specific issues with our parents, which can be unique to our particular story but universal in the fact that they affect our lives in the present.

When we start out on this very emotional exercise of letter writing, sometimes the first question a client has is a practical one: paper or computer? Typed or hand written? I encourage my clients to take the time and effort to write this letter out in their own handwriting. I think this letter writing exercise is a special, emotional experience that can be better appreciated when we actually write the words out in our own handwriting. Often times the process can be so emotional that we might find ourselves crying as we write this letter, a teardrop falling onto the page blurring the words, a powerful symbol of the process of emotional growth we are experiencing in these moments.

The hardest part of this exercise for many clients is the idea that in expressing their honest feelings about their child-hood they might hurt their parents' feelings. No matter how negatively the ways our parents raised us might have affected us, we often still love them and want to protect them from being hurt. We might seek to diminish their responsibility for their actions and instead take it upon ourselves to have acted or felt a different way in response to these actions. We make excuses for them. We take the blame. Part of the process of writing this letter is to free ourselves from the instinct to protect our parents, and instead be honest with them (and ourselves).

Eventually we reach the point where we discuss who this letter is really for. Is the letter really for the parent? It started out that way. But usually the real result of writing the letter is a feeling of accomplishment in the client after having transformed all this powerful emotional material from feelings into words. Turning all these unspoken, unidentified feelings into a physical object can have a transformative effect. We've taken these unspoken, mysterious emotions and gotten them out of ourselves. Often the client feels so much better after having written this letter, they wonder if they even need to send it to the parent. And I usually agree! The letter isn't really for the parent, it's for ourselves. In writing this letter we sometimes expect the parent to really understand us now, to see how the way they raised us might have affected us negatively, and thus feel sorry and want to apologize. However, that's taking the power to feel better about ourselves away from us and giving it to someone else. And it's unrealistic to think that a lifetime of behavior might be flipped on its head by one letter.

The whole point of the unsent letter is to empower ourselves to understand how our childhood affects us today. Once we are aware of that, we can work on ways to help us live happier lives. Having a parent understand us better and apologize for their actions might feel good, but that is usually a fantasy. We imagine that this apology will make us feel better, will enable us to live happier lives, but truly it is our newfound awareness of our adverse childhood experiences and how much they affect us in the present day that is going to make us feel better. For that reason, many times the client chooses not to send the letter and instead they keep it, or burn it, or stick it in a box in the garage and forget about it. The letter becomes a symbol, a marker of the before and after, the before being a time when we felt powerless and confused about the ways we act and feel in life that made us unhappy, and the after being a time when we understand why we act and feel in ways that make us unhappy, and can now develop clear goals based on this knowledge to help us live happier lives. The unsent letter represents a huge step we have taken in our own journey of personal growth, regardless of who reads it.

FORTY-TWO

Keeping a List

One my early clients was a writer who was sending out his latest screenplay to executives he knew. One of these executives was a woman who he had worked with before, and she had expressed interest in reading any other scripts the client had written. He sent her a friendly email, attached the script, and waited.

He didn't hear back from her that week. In our next session he expressed frustration. If she didn't have time read the script, she could at least send a reply saying she'd get to it soon. He grumbled about how maybe she didn't like him as much as he thought she did, and that maybe she didn't really enjoy working with him after all.

After two weeks without a response he was sure this woman secretly hated him, and had deleted his email as soon as she finished reading it, if she read it at all. The client couldn't imagine someone could go two weeks without replying to an email, not unless the person didn't want to deal with the person who had sent the email. The client mentioned that he had a list of executives he had sent the script off to, recording his correspondence and their reactions. He announced that he was crossing her name off the list. Good riddance!

This became a "hey, let's take a deep breath and relax before we make a decision" kind of moment. We examined the reality of the thoughts this client was having. He was doing something we call *projecting*, where he was taking the feelings he had about himself and his situation and assuming that this executive friend of his was thinking or feeling these same thoughts and emotions. He was also *catastrophizing*, imagining that the worst case scenario had happened. He had convinced himself that this woman hated him, that she thought he was a terrible writer and didn't want to deal with talking to him, and therefore she had ghosted him.

We decided that instead of acting right away and crossing her name off the list, the best thing to do would be to take a step back for a moment. Give the situation a little space. Don't make any more assumptions for the moment. He'd make a note to follow up in a week and forget about it until then. And so he did, but he didn't hear back. So he followed up after another week, but still didn't hear back. We worked on stop-ping his tendency to project and catastrophize, and instead stopped thinking about it. This process lasted for several weeks, and in later sessions the client mentioned wanting to send snarky or passive aggressive follow up emails, but realized that would only make things worse. Instead, he continued to send weekly follow up emails, friendly and polite without implying how frustrated he was with her communication with him, or trying to make her feel bad for making him feel this way. He simply said hello, just keeping in touch, get back to me when you can, hope you're well.

And a few weeks after that, he came into a session very excited. He had just gotten an email from the executive. She apologized for not replying to him sooner, saying how busy she has been with work, she got a promotion and also moved and is just now getting back into the swing of things. She also said she loved the script, and wanted to set a meeting to talk about it and catch up.

The takeaway for the client from this experience was to remember that other people don't always make their decisions based on you. They have their own timelines and priorities and emotional baggage, so when we imagine how they must think about us we are really just projecting how we think about ourselves. If we are sure that the person we're reaching out to hasn't responded because we're just not important enough to warrant a reply, then we must feel like we're not very important to anyone. We imagine other people have their own list, and perhaps we've been crossed off theirs, so we might as well cross them off of ours, right? Wrong! Stop keeping a list. In fact, stop thinking about crossing anybody off of anything!

FORTY-THREE

The House of Cards

A client I once worked with had experienced intense conflict with their mother regarding their sexuality. They had spent years of their life trying to reconcile this pain with their need to have a relationship with her, and finally gotten to the point where they felt like they were in a good place about it. They were learning to accept things as they were without permanent regret for how they could have been. Then one day over the holidays the mother went off on this client, making it crystal clear she would never accept their sexuality, their lifestyle, the person they had become. It was a crushing emotional blow for this client, who spent a therapy session processing this event, breaking into tears as they described the pain it had caused them. At the end of the session, feeling better after releasing these strong emotions, the client commented how it felt like their life was a house of cards that had come crashing to the ground, and now they had to start all over again, piece by piece, putting their life back together.

As we processed these feelings in further sessions we kept coming back to the house of cards metaphor. We talked about how we use this figure of speech to describe things as fragile, unreliable, apt to fall apart at any second. We dove deeper into the choice the client made in describing their life in this way, and how developing the power we have to change our lives can begin with something as simple as just describing things differently. We decided that fragile, unreliable, and apt to fall apart at any second were not ways in which this client wanted to continue to characterize their life.

Sometimes it's not so much about what happens in our lives as it is how we react to them. In this case, the client perceiving their life as a house of cards meant they were predisposed to interpret anything that happened to them as reflecting their fragile, unreliable life. I encouraged them to think about this moment in their life through a different lens. Instead of a house of cards, think about the classic road of life metaphor.

You've come far in life. You've dealt with issues, experienced relationships, struggled and succeeded, and gotten to the point where you are today. You've handled things that were difficult to handle and learned from the experience. But then something unexpected happens like what happened to this client. Something that throws everything in your life out of whack. It might feel like your life is a house of cards that has just collapsed, and you're shocked that the life you built could fall apart so easily. You feel unsafe and vulnerable. Your world has fallen apart.

Here's where we change our point of view. Instead of a house of cards collapsing, think of this moment in life as a car breaking down on the side of the road. You haven't fallen apart. Things haven't collapsed. You've simply stopped. You don't have to go back to square one. You get credit for how far you've come.

This turned out to be a valuable moment of realization for the client. The difference in how they felt about themselves through the prism of the house of cards metaphor versus the car breaking down metaphor was noticeable. With the house of cards, they thought of themselves as a failure, that all the work they had put into therapy was a waste, that it had all come crashing down and now the slow laborious task of putting it all together would begin. With the car metaphor, they felt more like they had encountered a setback that didn't necessarily ruin everything that had come before it. They were able to stop for a moment to assess how far they had come and how far they had to go, instead of feeling like their life had gone back to square one. The house of cards thought process felt like a dead end, where the car metaphor left them with a sense of hope. They began to feel like they could simply make some changes instead of starting all over, and continue down the road of life without such a feeling of disappointment.

Often times we talk about our lives using figures of speech as a short hand to describe the emotions we're feeling, but too often we make assumptions based on these figures of speech about the way we feel. If we strip away the metaphors and really examine the emotions we might find we can feel differently about things than we expected ourselves to be capable of. Sure, our rational mind knows life isn't really collapsing like a house of cards, but by referring to it like that we're reinforcing an emotional filter that's going to influence how we feel. Instead of something fragile and apt to come crashing down on us in moments of stress and trauma, think about life as something you're experiencing as a process. Sometimes it might seem like your life has collapsed and you have to struggle to put it back together, but the truth is your life is something you will always be working on. It's not a house of cards that can collapse, but instead a road trip that, even if we stop for breaks now and then, is always moving forwards.

FORTY-FOUR

We Are All Parents

I often tell clients that having children can be the cheapest (or most expensive) form of therapy. Learning to be a parent is a special experience, and at the same time there is the chance to learn to re-parent yourself. This chapter is not just for people with kids, it's for all of us, because each of us has a child we are raising: our inner child. By learning how to be a parent to that inner child, we can change our behavior to guide ourselves from unhappy, negative life patterns towards the positive types of relationships we want to experience.

The inner child refers to the nugget of our true selves that existed before we had a conscious idea of the concept of ourselves. It's a child who is pure and innocent and has not learned yet how to act, only to react. It's the part of ourselves that is driven by powerful emotions from the past that control the direction of our lives in the present. As we grow up and mature, finding meaning and a definition of ourselves in our relationships with friends, family, and romantic partners, we might look and talk like adults, but many of us don't always act like adults. Many of us aren't driven to act by the adult part of ourselves in ways that clearly and logically help the situations we are dealing with. We are in reality driven by the inner child, whose motivations are controlled more by emotions, the origins of which are often unclear, in ways that seem harmful or irrational regarding the situations we are dealing with at the time.

How can our lives be directed by the inner child in ways that run counter to what our adult selves actually want? It might be that our adult selves crave a relationship but our inner child is scared of intimacy, and makes sure we react with anger and skepticism to deeper emotional bonds, ensuring we don't engage in these relationships. Our adult selves might want a partner who respects us and loves us for who we are, but our inner child might have such strong feelings of shame and inadequacy that it drives us to stay in relationships with people who don't respect us and don't think about our needs and desires, protecting us from having to deal with the emotions a different kind of relationship might bring up. In these cases, our adult selves can have rational ideas about what we want and what's best for us, but our deeper emotions are controlled by our inner child.

An important part of our emotional growth is the separation between these two parts of ourselves. Once we recognize that what we want as adults can be in direct conflict with what our inner child wants, we can begin to differentiate between them. I encourage my clients to think about their inner child as a separate entity that they can interact with. I find it helpful to picture that inner child as the client at a young age, picking

out a memory or an old family photo to create a visual repre-
sentation of the child. Once we have that image, we can start
to identify the emotions that we assign to the inner child.
Emotions like anger, fear, jealousy, shame, and other powerful
feelings that can wash over us in stressful situations. Think
about identifying these situations and separating the person
feeling these emotions from you to the inner child, a situation
that generates feelings of inadequacy or shame, directing you
to feel like you're not capable of doing what you intend to do,
driving you to avoid or sabotage the situation in accordance to
these feelings instead of accepting the challenges head on in
the way your adult self is truly capable of. You might even
notice you feel these situations physically, with a rush of blood
to the head, a shameful blush, or a clenched jaw.

Now is the time to be the parent. Be your adult self, who is
mature, capable, and competent, and address your inner child,
who is ashamed, nervous, and afraid. Imagine giving your
inner child a hug, showing them the love and support that
would make you as an adult feel better. Sit that inner child on
your lap and talk to them. Tell them it's okay to feel the feelings they're feeling. Assure them that things happened in your
childhood that were out of their control and led them to have
the feelings they're having right now. Acknowledge that those
feelings might not be the most appropriate reaction to the situation that we, the adult, are dealing with.

Now take these skills and see if you're able to respond
differently to stressful or emotional situations in your daily life.
Hopefully the exercise of taking the reactive, negative
emotions off your shoulders and visualizing them as belonging
to your inner child will help you handle them differently. By

visualizing yourself as a parent you might find yourself acting and reacting in ways that are guided more by reason instead of deep seated emotions. By learning to parent your inner child, you will learn to love yourself. And as a bonus, you will be able to experience many of the positive aspects of being a parent without having to change any dirty diapers!

FORTY-FIVE

Teletherapy Pros and Cons

The idea of participating in talk therapy online has been around since technology became advanced enough to make it possible, but with the COVID pandemic and the drastic changes in our lives it caused, teletherapy has become a more attractive option for many people. I see many of my clients via teletherapy, and while some of them look forward to eventually getting back into the room in person, others are happy to continue to see me online. There are pros and cons to both options, and it's up to the individual to make their own decision, but the good news is that there is no wrong choice, only the decision that best reflects the preferences of the people involved.

The classic version of therapy, done in person, can be a transformative experience, and has many advantages over teletherapy. The most obvious one is the physical presence and connection between the client and the therapist in the room. The words we say mean a lot, but there is also a great deal of meaning in what we don't say, and which is expressed through our movements, our posture, how we present ourselves. There are also fewer distractions when you're sitting on a couch in an office as opposed to your couch at home. It's much more difficult to sneak a peek at your phone when you're sitting directly across from your therapist. Silence feels different when it's shared by two people sitting feet from each other, rather than each at their own computers. In addition, the act of physically going somewhere, sitting in the waiting room, and eventually entering the office is time that can be used to think about what will be discussed in that day's session. It can be a part of the therapy experience, the time before and after the session where we can process what we will talk about or have talked about. There is also a ritualistic aspect to in person therapy, as maybe there's a coffee shop or a bagel place nearby that one could look forward to. So on those days when you don't feel like going to therapy, at least you can have that extra motivation of a toasted everything bagel with cream cheese to keep you going!

The cons of in person therapy are fewer, but relevant. One is the idea of having to get into your car, or onto your bike, or public transportation, and physically go to on office. There's traffic to deal with, and the scheduling of that time around the other things going on in your life. These are factors that many people have become more aware of since the pandemic changes our lives so dramatically, and some people prefer not to return to the lifestyle they had lived pre-COVID. And while some people enjoy the idea of the therapy room as a sanctuary, other people might feel uncomfortable in what they perceive as an overly formal environment. There is also the additional consideration of geography. With in person therapy you are limited to finding a therapist physically close to you, while with teletherapy you can see a therapist anywhere in the state you live. (States have their own requirements regarding licensing therapists, one of which being that the client is required to be in the state where their therapist is licensed to work.) So, if you're looking for a therapist less than 10 miles from you, you will be more limited than if you have the entire state to choose from.

What are some of the pros about teletherapy? In my experience, the main one is the simple fact that you don't have to leave the house. Some people prefer being in their own environment, in what they feel is a more comfortable situation. They can log in from their own couch, or car, or on a break from work, or on a walk, anyplace where they have internet access and a certain amount of privacy. These factors tend to remove an air of formality from the whole process, from the idea that you have the power to log in from whatever location works best for you, to the fact that you don't have to wear shoes. Some clients have expressed that they feel more open to discussing sensitive or revealing topics in the comfort of their own home than they would in an office setting. For new clients who might have been on the fence about starting talk therapy, the idea that they can log in at their own (relative) convenience can be the tipping point that gets them to give it a try. There's also less of an investment of time when you don't have to physically go somewhere to see what it's like, and you've spent less time going to and coming back from the appointment in the way you would have if you were seeing a therapist in person, both of which can make it easier to try.

Even with all these pros about teletherapy, there are still a good number of cons to consider. One of the main ones is that it's such a drastic change from how therapy has always been conducted. The fact that the client and therapist are not physically in a room together brings up not just practical technological issues but emotional issues about the nature of therapy and the relationship between client and therapist. Some therapists and clients consider teletherapy to be inadequate compared to in person therapy. This might play out in the very things that we previously discussed as pros; namely, in the formality of the setting. Sometimes we need to be put in an uncomfortable position in order to be moved to explore uncomfortable topics. We might be more likely to feel like we don't want to get too deep or explore uncomfortable topics when we're enjoying the comfort of our own home. It is also much harder to connect as people when we're doing it across computer screens. Eye contact can be difficult to maintain, body language can be difficult to assess, and just the fact that we're looking at a person's image on a tiny box on a screen as opposed to a real person in person can have an adverse affect on the clinical experience. Throw in the chances of a bad internet connection, choppy audio, or unanticipated technical difficulties and we see there are certainly some hurdles to a successful teletherapy experience.

In my opinion, the best course of action regarding in person therapy vs teletherapy is to to try it one way, and if you don't like it, try it the other way. I've experienced both situations as a therapist and as a client. I value the time I spent going into my therapist's office in person, and I also value the time I spend with my clients via teletherapy. You might find that older, more established therapists prefer to work in person, while younger, less established therapists are more open to teletherapy. Of course, you might also find therapists that defy the expectations you have of them based on assumptions about their age or experience. The most important thing is to find a therapist that you click with, whatever the setting. In one situation you might get a bagel and cream cheese after your session, and in the other you might not be wearing shoes, but either way you can still have a rewarding therapy experience.

FORTY-SIX

Say It (Out) Loud

Talk therapy is a process through which we learn more about ourselves. But don't we already know everything about ourselves? After all, we've been right there by our own side throughout our entire lives. We've lived through all our childhood experiences, we were there for everything our parents told us, we remember the decisions we made growing up, the events that shaped us, we witnessed it all. So what's the point of talking about things we already know?

The answer is, we don't always know as much as we think. And even though we know something, we might not *really* know it. We might remember it, how it felt, how it feels now when we think about it, but not really consider how it continues to affect our lives. We might remember how hard it was to lose a parent at an early age, but we might not truly appreciate how much that event continues to affect our lives until we start to describe how we felt at the time, and how we feel about it now. We might think we know how we feel about an abusive event or traumatic experience that happened earlier in our lives, but after talking about it in the present we might realize we have been downplaying the event and its aftermath when all along it had a much greater psychological impact on ourselves than we thought. We might think we know why our previous relationships haven't worked out the way we wanted, but only by talking about them in more detail can we realize that the relationship modeling we saw from our own parents made it inevitable that our future relationships would follow the same pattern. Saying these things out loud brings them out of the subconscious shadows and into the open, where we can appreciate their effects on our adult lives.

Sometimes there is a lot of resistance to talking about painful events from the past. A client might be discussing the impact of anxiety regarding work on their lives and mention something their father did that made them feel a similar way. This, to the therapist, is a clue, a marker on the path that leads to where the real issue lies. But when asked to describe more about their father and the origin of these anxious feelings, the client might avoid talking about it. This could take the form of minimizing the impact of these early events, a claim that they happened so long ago the client barely remembers anything about them, or a straightforward statement by the client that they don't want to delve deeper into the topic. So, we will circle around this painful area, talking about the present day results of it, and not go any deeper. However, the therapist will take note of the resistance to talking about the father's actions regarding anxiety and the fact that they seem to have affected the client so strongly as to make them resistant to revisiting those feelings. This area of resistance will be revisited, delicately, with the knowledge that in this area of discussion are the painful feelings that we want to uncover in order to examine how they might be directing the way we act and feel in our current lives. It is one thing to know that our father was an angry man who took out that anger on the people around him, and that we learned to adapt to it and deal with it. It is another thing to say out loud "My dad made me feel like I was stupid, like I couldn't do anything right, and now when I am made to feel stupid as an adult I get furious". That physical act of saying the words forces us to acknowledge them in a way that just thinking about them does not.

That is another powerful result of saying things out loud: it forces us to acknowledge them. Traumatic events or painful memories are things we spend much of our adults lives trying to suppress, but the truth is that by doing this we allow them to live on in the background, influencing our actions and guiding our lives from behind the scenes. Naming these things, taking the time to really delve into them, shines a light on them in a way that will make us more aware of their influence. It can be quite a shock to realize that an event that we had convinced ourselves wasn't really a big deal is actually a much bigger deal that we could have ever thought. And what is it that can lead us to have this realization? Talking about it. Saying it out loud.

That is the power of words, of saying things out loud. What do we say when confronted with an ugly truth we don't want acknowledge? A painful event we don't want to relive? A memory laced with guilt and shame we've spent a lifetime minimizing? We say we don't want to talk about it. And that is directly related to the whole point of talk therapy: We learn to talk about things that are painful to talk about. For some people it can take a long time to get comfortable enough to engage with these painful memories. For other people, they might have come to therapy ready to talk, bursting with the desires to discuss these traumatic events. Still other people might not even know they have been avoiding talking about a particular subject until the subject comes up. The point is, it is only once we commit to verbalizing the feelings that are making us unhappy that we can truly begin to understand them. Only after we have done that can we begin the work of learning how these things we avoided talking about are affecting our lives, and how we can learn to accept them. Saying It Out Loud is the whole point of talk therapy; to process painful emotions from the past we've spent our lives avoiding, breaking their control on us in the present, and giving ourselves the chance to live happier lives.

FORTY-SEVEN

The Record Grooves of Change

"Okay, I see what's causing the problem. Now, how do I change it?" It's a happy moment when I hear a client say this. It marks a level of self-awareness that exhibits the kind of emotional growth one can experience through the process of talk therapy. It often comes after a good amount of introspection and analysis regarding what the client sees as the difficulties in their life. An honest assessment of what they want and what's standing in their way of getting it. For this chapter, let's use as an example someone who is experiencing unhappiness in their relationship with their partner. What they say they want is to have a happy, loving relationship, to have things be easy, without any conflict or stress. The problem is, right now things are definitely not easy, and there is lots of conflict and stress. This all seems to be part of a cycle of unhappiness they can't seem to break out of. They acknowledge they are unhappy, that they want things to change, and are willing to work at making this happen. But how? Here's how this process might play out in talk therapy.

We would probably start out by discussing a fight the client recently had with their partner. We'd talk about the play by play of what happened and explore why the client felt and acted the way they did. We won't come up with any solutions right away, but we'll dig deeper into both the partner's role and the client's role in the conflict. We might learn that what the partner did or said triggered something inside the client that caused fear or anxiety, and that this caused the client to become angry and direct that anger towards their partner in a way that was out of proportion to what the partner actually said or did. Or vice versa. The client will be encouraged to consider all this the next time a similar fight comes up.

And a similar fight always comes up. And then the process plays out in subsequent sessions. Play by play, analysis, intro- spection. With each session we continue to identify the patterns in the client's behavior. Often times we start out talking about the client's partner and what they do to instigate or escalate these fights, but eventually we get to the point where we spend more time talking about the client's actions and feelings. We might examine the client's emotional material behind their actions, including their childhood, their relation- ships with their parents or caregivers, any past trauma that might have an influence on the situation, and their past rela- tionship experiences.

At some point we will become able to identify the origin of the anger, fear, and other strong emotions causing the rela- tionship conflict. Hopefully it will come in a moment of clar- ity, a light bulb moment, something along the lines of "Ah! I get it now. The fact that my partner doesn't scrape enough food off the dishes before putting them in the dishwasher and it ends up getting crusted on after it dries isn't a personal attack on me, but it triggers emotions related to my relationship with my mother, who was so concerned with cleanliness that if I didn't conform to her way of thinking I wouldn't receive love, so I learned that cleanliness is a way to express love, so when my partner doesn't have the same attitude towards cleanliness as me I take that as a denial of love". Or something like that.

So now we've identified the true cause of the relationship conflict. It turns out it wasn't the partner's actions, it was the childhood emotional material triggered by their partner's actions. Clients verbalize these kind of realizations in different ways, but the common thread is a feeling of pride and excitement about achieving this level of emotional awareness. It shows that the work they've put into therapy so far has paid off. It's an example of how powerful self awareness can be. Of course, very quickly that feeling of satisfaction becomes a desire to go further. Now the question becomes: How do I change?

This is where the concept of the record grooves come in. A record is designed to sound the same way every time, as the grooves guide the needle in a predetermined direction. The way we behave in relationships can be thought of in the same way. Our personalities have grooves, and when the needle of relationship drama drops on us we react in a certain way. We play a certain song. The same song we've always played. The grooves of this song are cut early in our lives, shaped by our childhood experiences, and grow slowly over the course of our lives, their edges getting higher, eventually becoming canyons that can be very hard to break out of.

So how do we change? With repetition. Through our work in therapy we will eventually wear down the grooves of the client's song. Think of the typical fight our client has with their partner about cleanliness like it's a song. We'll analyze how this song sounds, what the song is really about, and question why we're listening to this song in the first place. We examine the root causes of the song, including who taught us this song, who taught them this song, and what's the point of this particular song in the first place? Through this line of thinking we begin to wear down the grooves to the point where eventually the record skips, and all of a sudden we're listening to a different song.

As this process plays out the client becomes especially aware of the emotions behind their actions. It becomes second nature for them to think about why they're reacting the way they do instead of just reacting mindlessly. It's like we have become detectives, seeing clues about our behavior and emotions we weren't able to see before, and now we're putting the clues together to see the whole picture. And then, quite often, there is another wonderful moment in the therapeutic process. To continue with our record analogy, this is the record scratch moment. The client might report that they were in a situation with their partner recently that in the past would have resulted in a fight between them, the same old song playing again, but instead this time the record scratched, the song changed, and they found themselves handling the situation differently. There was less anger or fear than they typically experience, and more of a sense of calm and normalcy.

Things that were in the past a big deal are now not such a big deal. Often times the partner notices this too, and comments on how the client is acting differently, and for the better. It's a moment of success, a happy day when the client is able to appreciate that "somehow" they were able to react differently.

I put "somehow" in quotes because at this point it feels easy for the client. "Somehow" they just felt differently and acted differently and there was a different outcome, and they are happier for it. Of course, this "somehow" actually consists of all the time we spent up until this point talking about the fights, the family history, the struggles, the fear, listening to the song that they had been playing their whole lives. The hours of talking and questioning and self examination now make perfect sense, because they have led us to the point where we are finally able to change. It is the hard work of talk therapy to wear down the grooves of our own personal records, and realize we have the power to choose to hear a different song.

FORTY-EIGHT

Asking All the (Right?) Questions

There is a particular therapy related stereotype that often comes up when people describe their experiences with therapists. It usually happens when the client has expressed something and, in trying to process it, asks the therapist what they think. The response in this stereotypical conversation is something like "What do <u>you</u> think?". This always elicits a groan, as whenever someone asks a question they expect an answer in return, not another question. It's related to the thing that happens when a client is confronted with certain questions about what to do in their lives, and they ask the therapist for the answers. When this happens to me, I tell clients that I don't have the answers, but I do have the questions. How annoying is that?

We don't get asked questions in our everyday lives like we do in therapy. In real life you might be asked "What's the matter?", or "What's wrong?". These questions certainly indicate that someone in your life cares about you, which is nice, but because those people care about you they're going to stop asking questions when you start to show some resistance. When things get awkward. When you react in a way that seems upset or annoyed. However, in therapy it's part of the therapist's job to focus in on this resistance. It means we're on the right path, that we're getting close to topics that the client doesn't want to acknowledge or explore, and which ironically are the ones that the most personal growth can be gained from acknowledging and exploring. In our personal relationships these questions are stop signs, but in our therapeutic relationships we see the stop signs as green lights, guiding us to where the real issues lie.

This method of asking questions instead of giving answers has its root with Socrates, an old Greek guy. His style of teaching involved asking students questions that would spur them to think for themselves and find their own answers. It is in this tradition that therapists ask questions of their clients that lead them to learn about their problems and solutions without the therapist telling them what they think about their problems and solutions.

If you're thinking that talk therapy sounds like a weekly interrogation session, you should know that it's not. I ask questions of my clients not to put them on the spot, but to probe and test and feel out what the issues that affect them the most are. When I encounter resistance, I don't push. If someone really doesn't want to answer a question that will lead to them talking about something sensitive that they're not ready to confront yet, I can put a pin in it and circle back. And at some point I'm definitely going to circle back. Many times people come to therapy to talk about things they are not yet ready to talk about. Sometimes there are issues that deep down they know the truth about, but admitting them to another person makes them tangible in a way that is scary. Many times the client, after having been asked a question and avoiding it, will come back in later sessions and be ready to talk about it, after having experience such resistance to direct questioning and processing how they reacted and why.

Sometimes these questions are so simple they seem juvenile, because at first the answers are simple. They are more cause and effect. But as we get into further questions we eventually are forced to confront the real reasons behind why we do the things we do. Why did you yell at your coworker like that? Because he did X or Y or Z. Yes, but why did you yell at him? Because I was angry, I just told you he did X or Y or Z. What about that made you angry? Hm… OR - Why did you ignore your partner when they asked you to do X or Y or Z? Because it was a stupid thing to ask. Okay, but why did you ignore them about it? Because they know I didn't want to do it. I see. Why didn't you just tell them that instead of ignoring them? Because… Hm… Both of these scenarios end with a beginning. A stop to the automatic replies and a moment of deeper thought. Now we're getting somewhere!

If you have or are going to experience talk therapy, you should be prepared to answer some questions. If you start to get annoyed or angry about this process, think about why. Sure, it might be annoying in general for someone to ask you a bunch of questions, but is your reaction really to the questions? Or is it to the answers? Because the answers are already inside you, whether we're ready to deal with them or not.

FORTY-NINE

The Weight We Carry

W e live in a culture that places a great value on how we look. There's a lot of pressure on our appearance, especially our weight, that can result in us searching for ways to lose that weight, whether by diet, exercise, or other means. We might get into a pattern of stepping on the scale every morning and having that number be a determining factor in whether we feel good or bad about ourselves. We might focus on our diet or our exercise program in ways that change them from being about living a healthy lifestyle to being intensely focused on doing every little thing we can to get that number on the scale down the next morning. In a physical sense we can be very conscious of our weight, but there is another kind of weight that affects us even more: emotional weight.

Emotional weight is what we feel when we're too depressed to drag ourselves out of bed in the morning. It's what we feel when we start out worrying about the implications of traffic causing us to be late to work and end up worrying that we're going to die alone. It's what we feel when we cycle through the same angry arguments in our romantic relationships every time we go out to dinner. It's what we feel when we deal with our parents getting older and become more dependent on us to the point where we start to resent them. Emotional weight refers to the feelings we carry with us, feelings that guide us unconsciously into patterns of behavior that make us unhappy, even though consciously we know they make us unhappy.

When I'm working with a client who indicates they're in this type of situation, I try to ease into using this kind of symbolism. We might talk about how the client is carrying a lot of emotions with them, how they must feel like they have a lot of weight on their shoulders, how their situation sounds really heavy. We might talk about how they feel like they have a lot of baggage, which is another way we relate emotional trauma to physical presence. All this talk is a way to start to think about these internal emotions as something more external. We get to the point where we can clearly identify these cycles of depression, or loss, or anxiety, or anger, any of these feelings that are present and recurring and causing them unhappiness. Then we talk about using a specific image of a weight that we can imagine pointing at and observing. A giant barbell, a huge sack of potatoes, a backpack full of books, anything the client chooses. And then we get to work.

This work is all about identifying the source of the weight. We talk about putting down the weight in the middle of the therapy room and observing it without feeling the burden of carrying it for the moment. We might talk about the history of the weight, how it started, how it has grown, how much of a part of the client's life it has become. We would also discuss the things the client can do to eliminate the weight. Proactive, concrete steps we can identify that would lessen the burden. And as we talk about the weight in an external sense, the client might, for the moment, feel relieved of the burden. The irony is, as we sit and pay attention to the origins and effects of the weight, we might find ourselves feeling light and unburdened because even though we're addressing it, we don't feel like we're carrying it. This is the work of talk therapy, the processing of emotions to better understand them and in the process diminish their control over our lives.

This process is not a one session fix. It can take time to identify and engage in the various steps laid out here. In fact, just getting to the point where we recognize we are carrying a weight can take some time. However, once we get to the point where we identify the weight and really analyze it, we are on the path to change. With many clients, we reach a point where they will come into session one day with an excited demeanor, eager to express something that happened in the past week. They might have found themselves in a situation that in the past would have caused them to react with feelings of sadness or resentment or shame or anger, but instead they reacted differently. They didn't go to the dark place where in the past they would have gone. They felt better about themselves. In fact, they feel like (drumroll please)… A weight has been lifted off their shoulders!

FIFTY

The Ugly Light Fixture

I once worked with a client who lived by herself in an apartment. Her presenting problem (reason for seeking therapy) was that she was feeling stuck and unhappy with her life. As we got to know each other, we often talked about her apartment. When she moved in a few years prior, she was excited to decorate the place to her own liking after having roommates for many years. She got to work arranging furniture, hanging art, making the place feel like home. Over the course of her first year living there it started to feel like home. Except for one thing she disliked: an ugly light fixture.

The ugly light fixture was there when she moved in, right in the entry way, the first thing you saw when you entered the apartment. It was made of glass but it was cloudy, it looked dirty, and a little crooked, like it had been attached poorly and not properly adjusted. She never liked it, and she always felt a pang of anxiety whenever she saw it. She never really considered changing it though, for various reasons. She didn't think of herself as being handy enough to change it, she was scared to deal with anything electrical, and she didn't want to deal with the work of finding an electrician to change it out and spend the money to have it done. So she lived with it. As everything else in her apartment changed over the years to reflect her taste and personality, the ugly light fixture remained. Every time she walked into the apartment and turned on the light, she saw the fixture and felt a little bad. This bad feeling was composed of disgust for the aesthetic ugliness of it, but also the shame she felt for allowing it to be there when she knew she didn't like it, and then disappointment in herself for not changing it, and as a result guilt for not being the kind of person who addresses these things. This light fixture had some serious emotional power in her life!

Time went by, and life went on. Eventually she started to lose interest in her job and started to feel lost. She was unhappy being single and envied her friends who had coupled off and gotten married. In short, she was in a rut. We discussed these feelings in therapy, and one thing that came up was her feelings about her apartment. How when she moved in she had been excited about it, but that now it felt like a part of her stuck-ness. We ended up talking all about the ugly light fixture. She started to feel like it symbolized her stuck-ness. As she spoke about this realization she got more and more animated. By the time we were done she was ready to act.

Later that day she went home, flipped on the light switch, and scrutinized the ugly light fixture. She thought about all the reasons why she had never done anything about it, which as she was thinking about them realized they weren't actually reasons, they were feelings. Something inside her clicked. She was ready to do something about it.

She picked up her phone and Yelped an electrician and explained the problem. The electrician was available to come by later that afternoon.

She looked online for stores in her neighborhood that sold light fixtures, and went and bought one.

She got home just in time to meet the electrician, who took off the old light fixture, replaced the bulb, and put up the new light fixture.

And it looked great!

After the electrician left, she stood in her kitchen, beaming. She was amazed that one little act could make her feel so good. And it only took an hour to change what she'd been feeling for years. She walked around the apartment, doing things she had always done there, only in a whole new light.

From that day on, every time she came home to her apartment and flipped on the light she smiled and felt good about herself. And these feelings started to bleed into other parts of her life. She began to actively work to change things in her life she didn't like. This included a reassessment of her career, which led to changes that she felt improved her life and made her happier and more engaged. She was more open to changes in her life in general, and started to look forward to them. In short, the work we did in therapy helped her identify something in her life that symbolized her larger problems, and she was able to do something about it to make herself happier.

I think we all have things in our lives like this client's ugly light fixture. Small, nagging things that we don't like but keep in our lives as if to torture ourselves. They seem like no big deal. On the surface, they're not. But they are a barrier that protects us from having to do something we don't want to do: change. We fear the change that would result if we fix these things. We might feel like we're not capable of making these changes, or that we don't deserve the improvements these changes might bring about. For some reason, it's part of our nature to build roadblocks for ourselves that prevent us from having to deal with change, whether or not that change will ultimately be good for us.

These roadblocks are of our own making, and it is in our own power to change them. It's usually scary and hard, but worth engaging. The small steps in life prepare us for the big ones. Take stock of your own life, see if you have your own ugly light fixture, and change it!

Additional Resources

Psychology Today and Therapy Den are both great resources with all kinds of information about mental health, including a search feature where you can look for a mental health professional near you.

https://www.psychologytoday.com/us

https://www.therapyden.com

If you're interested in learning more about mindfulness, here are several links to get you started.

https://www.mindful.org/everyday-mindfulness-with-jon-kabat-zinn/

https://www.psycom.net/mental-health-wellbeing/meditation-resources

https://www.healthline.com/health/mental-health/top-meditation-iphone-android-apps

Didi Hirsch Mental Health Services is known for their suicide prevention programs, so if you or someone you know are having thoughts of self harm or suicide, they are a good resource to reach out to.

https://didihirsch.org

My website is where you can find my contact information and social media links in case you're interested in sharing any questions, comments, opinions, suggestions, or recipes.

https://www.starktalk.net

A Note on Confidentiality

Confidentiality is a cornerstone of talk therapy. People need to feel safe enough to reveal their innermost thoughts with the knowledge that nobody besides their therapist will ever hear them, and this is a practice I take very seriously. Throughout this book there are instances where I refer to working with clients and our discussions in session, but these scenarios are hypothetical, and invented in order to illustrate the concept being considered, not the experience of any specific person. In all cases details have been changed to protect the confidentially of everyone involved.

A Note on Typos

I have purposely inserted several typos and grammatical errors at various places in this book. If you find one, please email me at DWMCtypos@gmail.com, notify me of the typo or grammatical error, and I will send you an email of thanks, along with one dollar. If the typo or grammatical error has already been found you will not get an email from me, nor one dollar, but thanks anyways for participating.